By
Gordon Corrigan

Introduction

As the shelves of Waterstones and the television schedules testify, large sections of the British public are fascinated by military history, and it may be apposite to enquire why. After all, who cares who won the Battle of Beni Boo Ali?[*] Or when the Battle of Vinegar Hill was fought?[†] Is anyone really interested in who fought who in the Whisky Wars,[‡] or in the frontier campaigns of Tiglath Pileser III?[§] Particularly as we British consider ourselves to be a peaceful people, slow to anger and abhorring violence, only resorting to military action when all other means of conflict resolution have been exhausted. That being so, it may be somewhat difficult to explain why, in the 957 years since the Norman Conquest, England and later Britain has been at war for 578 of those years, or for rather more than sixty percent of our entire history since 1066. In case anyone might think that this figure is distorted by medieval dynastic squabbles and civil wars, it may be worth pointing out that in the twentieth century, British troops were in action for eighty of those hundred years, and I count only those campaigns for which a medal was awarded – if we count all periods of active service then the figure would be even greater.

As to whom we were fighting during those 578 years, it was just about everybody, and often several campaigns simultaneously on opposite sides of the globe. We spent only twenty-four years fighting the Germans,[**] historically generally our allies, fifty-four years fighting the Spanish, fifty-two years fighting the Scots and

---

[*] The British Indian Army in 1821 v rebellious tribesmen in Muscat.
[†] 1798. British troops v Irish rebels.
[‡] US troops v illegal whisky distillers in 1869.
[§] King of Assyria 745 – 727 BC, the architect of Assyrian expansion.
[**] Two world wars and the War of the Spanish Succession 1701 – 1714 when there were German states on both sides.

196 years fighting the French.[*] Statistically, therefore, one year in every five we go to war with France. It is no wonder that they do not like us. It is perhaps inevitable that two nations on either side of a narrow piece of water, both with global ambitions, both dependent on trade and, later, both intent on creating a colonial empire, should be in competition with each other, either militarily, economically or politically. There were those in Britain in the run up to the First World War who thought the UK should side with Germany against France and Russia, blind to the fact that the only reason Germany could have for creating a blue water navy would be to take on the Royal Navy at some time in the future. There were even those who felt in the 1930s that allowing Hitler's Germany free rein in Europe while Britain concentrated on her empire as a sea power, would better serve British interests than going to war beside an enfeebled and morally bankrupt France.

That historical enmity could have been, and indeed often was, the cause of friction on the two occasions when Britain and France were on the same side, in the Crimean War (1854-57) and the First World War 1914-18. In the Crimea the British commander in chief, Fitzroy Somerset, Lord Raglan, constantly referred to the French when he meant the enemy, having to be reminded by his staff that the enemy were the Russians, and that on this rare occasion the French were allies. In fairness to Raglan, he had been on Wellington's staff for most of the Peninsula War, fighting the French, and lost an arm at Waterloo. There was not much cause to exchange maps in the Crimea, but in 1914 the methods of map marking could have caused confusion, to say the least. When marking one's own and enemy positions on a map the British convention was to show friendly forces in red, because traditionally British soldiers had worn red, and enemy forces in blue, because the enemy was generally French, and they wore blue. The French convention was exactly the reverse, for the same reason. As the British army on the Western Front was smaller than

---

[*] In the Hundred Years War only those periods of actual fighting are included.

2

that of the French, the British changed, and to this day friendly forces are blue and enemy red.

The longest of the many wars fought between England (Britain after Scotland joined the Union in 1707) and France was The Hundred Years War, actually lasting one hundred and sixteen years from 1337 to 1453. It was not a constant period of fighting, rather a series of campaigns separated by periods of relative peace or truces, some of them quite long. In that the English aims were consistent throughout the period, it is reasonable to consider it as one war, albeit no one who took part in the opening campaigns was alive at the close. Its ostensible cause was England's claim to the French throne as of right; the real cause was the wish to regain lands originally held in what is now France but lost over the centuries.

France at the time of the war was not the unified country that we know today. Only the Isle de France, the area around Paris, was ruled directly by the French king. The rest was a number of duchies with a large amount of autonomy, ruled by dukes who owed fealty to the king. However, that fealty was only enforceable when the king was strong and rich: otherwise, the dukes could do pretty much as they liked,

It was a war between a socially mobile England that was developing a new way of waging war, and a rigidly stultified feudal system which found it almost impossible to adapt. This saw tiny English armies consistently defeat far larger French ones, and even when the beaten commanders knew full well why they had lost, they were unable to develop countermeasures. In the end, of course, weight of population, deep pockets and political instability in England caused the withdrawal of English armies from Europe[*], in 1453, but the war did turn Anglo-Normans into Englishmen, and men of Artois, Gascony, Burgundy and Anjou into Frenchmen.

There were three great battles during the period, conducted by three great warriors, battles which even today are well known to

---

[*] Except for Calais, held until captured by the French is a surprise attack in 1558.

most Britons: Crécy in 1346 (Edward III), Poitiers in 1356 (the Black Prince) and Agincourt in 1415 (Henry V). The first major naval battle was the less well-known Battle of Sluys, which is the subject of a separate work.[*] This book deals with Crécy, its background, and its aftermath.

---

[*] Corrigan, Gordon, England Expects: The Battle of Sluys, ASIN: B07B2JZ3XP, Sharpe Books, London, 2018.

Chapter One – How it All Began

It all started with William the Bastard, Stamping Billy, William of Normandy, who conquered England in 1066, although it did take a few years to pacify the entire country. Edward the Confessor, King of England and the last king of the House of Wessex, died childless in 1066. The Anglo-Saxon royal succession did not depend on primogeniture, as it does today, although it usually went to someone in the same extended family. While the king could express a preference as to who should succeed him, the final decision was made by the Witan, a council of elders selected from among the great men of the realm. What was important was that the successor must be 'throne worthy' which usually meant an adult in full possession of his faculties and able to command the support of the magnates.

Edward died on 5 February 1066 and Harold Godwinson, Harold II, proclaimed by the Witan, succeeded him, and was crowned the following day. Harold claimed that Edward on his deathbed had vouchsafed the crown to him. There were other possible claimants, the strongest by blood being Edgar, grandson of King Edmund Ironside, but he was a child, and so not 'throne worthy'. William of Normandy did have a blood claim, in that he was Edward's first cousin once removed, and also maintained that he had been promised the crown by Edward and that Harold had promised to uphold that claim. Harold, Earl of Wessex, on the other hand, was the most powerful man in the kingdom, despite having no royal blood, although his sister had been Edward the Confessor's queen.

Harold was certainly not one to shirk his military responsibilities. Had he not rushed north to defeat an invasion led by Harold Hardrada, the King of Norway, and supported by his own brother, Tostig, he might have been able to defeat William of Normandy's invasion on the beaches, and English and European history would be different. As it was William landed unopposed. Harold defeated the northern invasion at the Battle of Stamford Bridge, where both Harold Hardrada and Tostig were killed, but by the time he heard of William's landing and force marched back down south it was too late. Harold Godwinson was killed, and with him died Anglo-Saxon England.

Although there were uprisings against William, they were uncoordinated and badly planned, and William had no great difficulty in putting them down. Anglo-Saxon aristocracy disappeared, Anglo-Saxon landowners were dispossessed, and all Anglo-Saxon bishops were dethroned except one, replaced by Norman vassals of William. By the 1070s castles had been built all over the country and secure within their walls French speaking Normans ruled over Old English-speaking Saxons. By the time of the completion of the Domesday Book in 1086, only two Anglo-Saxons are named as having holdings of any significance. It was the greatest upheaval in English society, law and religion since the Roman withdrawal in the early 5th Century.

Now the ruling classes held lands on both sides of the Channel, which was fine as long as their feudal overlord was the same person in England as he was in Normandy. This was the case until William I's death in 1087,[*] when his eldest son Robert became Duke of Normandy while his third son (the second had been killed in a hunting accident) became King of England as William II 'Rufus'.[†] There was no attempt to combine the two territories into one, so now the great magnates had a problem, for when William and Robert were opposed, as they often were, cleaving to one Lord meant alienating the other. This situation was not resolved until Robert went crusading financed by money advanced by William against the stewardship of Normandy. William Rufus was killed in a hunting accident in 1100 to be succeeded by his brother, the Conqueror's fourth son, Henry I. By then Maine and much of the Vexin (that area between Rouen and Paris) had been added to English holdings. Henry was no great soldier, but he did manage to take Normandy from his returned-from-crusade brother Robert,

---

[*] He died in Rouen and is buried in the Abbaye aux Hommes in Caen, although after subsequent desecrations of the grave only one thigh bone is believed to be in the tomb there now.
[†] Probably so called because of his ruddy complexion, although some say that he had red hair.

and he did manage to govern England and Normandy for thirty-five years, avoiding revolt by a judicious mixture of terror, reward, and shrewd financial management. Although Henry had numerous illegitimate children, he only produced one legitimate son, who drowned when his ship went down in 1120. His attempts to persuade the barons to accept his daughter Matilda as his successor as queen regnant failed spectacularly. The great men of the kingdom might have accepted Matilda, the widow of the Holy Roman Emperor and hence usually referred to as 'the Empress', but they were not going to accept her second husband, Geoffrey of Anjou. They awarded the throne instead to Stephen of Blois, Duke of Normandy, a nephew of Henry I and grandson of the conqueror through his daughter Adela – and confusingly also married to a Matilda, this time of Boulogne. The result was a prolonged period of instability and vicious civil war, known to at least one contemporary chronicler as 'the time when God slept'. It was only resolved when the English Church brokered peace, and it was agreed in the Treaty of Westminster in 1153 that Stephen should be succeeded on his death by Henry II, the son of Empress Matilda and Geoffrey of Anjou.

Henry II was already immensely rich and a holder of extensive lands when he came to the throne. In addition to Normandy, he had inherited Anjou, Maine and Touraine from his father and three years before coming to the throne had married Eleanor, Duchess of Aquitaine, who had inherited the duchy from her father who had no sons. Eleanor had been married at the age of fifteen to Louis VII, King of France, but after fifteen years the marriage was annulled. Officially this was on the grounds of consanguinity, but presumably because while she had produced two daughters there was no sign of a son. Only two months later she married Henry, which was seen by the French as an insult to their king. By the time Stephen died in 1154[*] and Henry became king, he was

---

[*] He was buried in Faversham Abbey, which he had founded, and which was destroyed shortly after the dissolution of the monasteries in 1538. It is said that his bones were reinterred in the local parish church where there is a tomb purporting to be his.

recognised as the overlord of Scotland and most of Ireland, and when he added Brittany to his fiefdoms, he held more of France than their own king did.

Henry II is mostly remembered in British history for his disputes with Thomas Becket, one time Chancellor of England and subsequently Archbishop of Canterbury. These disputes included the question of 'criminous clerks' – persons in holy orders who committed civil offences could only be tried by an ecclesiastical court which could not impose the death penalty. Henry thought they should be defrocked and handed over for trial by the civil administration. They were also at odds over the appointment of bishops, Becket's feudal duty to provide men at arms or cash in lieu for the king's military adventures, and Becket's objections to the crowning of Henry's son and heir (also a Henry) during his father's lifetime (the only occurrence in English history). Although Becket may well have deserved all he got, and certainly seems to have gone out of his way to provoke his own assassination, it was probably not at the king's instigation – although to this day Canterbury Cathedral continues to attract tourist dollars to view the site of the killing.

Henry said himself that he ruled by 'force of will and hard riding', for in an age without instant communications and the mass media, medieval kings had to be seen and had to move around their lands to enforce the law and keep over-mighty subjects in check. In the thirty-five years of his reign, Henry spent twenty-one of them in his continental possessions, for it was there that he was threatened, rather than in a united England which was now mainly a source of revenue. A mere twenty years later nearly all of Henry's empire would be lost, and it was the memory of that empire that would provide one of the provocations for the Hundred Years War.

Henry II's intention was that his eldest son, also Henry, would become King of England while his second surviving son, Richard, would inherit his mother's lands and titles in Aquitaine and Poitiers. When Prince Henry died of dysentery in 1183 the king assumed that as Richard was now the heir apparent, Aquitaine would pass to his third son, John. Richard, however, having learnt his trade as a soldier subduing rebellious barons there, had no intention of giving up Aquitaine. Family quarrels, culminating in an 1189 invasion of England by Richard supported by the French king, Philip II, forced King Henry to make a humiliating peace shortly before he died, leaving the thirty-two year old Richard as king. Although he has gone down in legend as Richard the Lion Heart, the great warrior king of England and chivalrous knight par excellence, in his ten years on the throne he spent only six months in England. Coming back from a crusade he was captured by Duke Leopold of Austria, sold on to the Holy Roman Emperor and held prisoner for a year while a 'king's ransom' of 100,000 marks was raised to free him. A mark was eight ounces of silver, so the ransom was roughly equivalent to around £15 million in silver prices today, raised in the main by a twenty-five percent tax on all rents and on the value of all moveable property, both in England and in Normandy, and that from a total population of around three million.

During Richard's absence on crusade, and then in prison, the French had made considerable inroads into the English domains on the continent. From 1194 Richard spent most of his time in Europe recovering the lost lands and castles, and building new defence works – notably Chateau Gaillard, which to this day looms 300 feet above the River Seine – to protect them. Then, at a little-known and militarily insignificant skirmish at Chalus, twenty miles south-west of Limoges, Richard sustained a wound from a crossbow bolt, which went septic and from which he died on 6 April 1199, aged forty-two. As his marriage to Berengaria of Navarre was childless, he was succeeded by his brother John.

John has not been treated kindly by history. As a younger son who rebelled against his father, sided with the French in an invasion of England, spectacularly failed as governor of Ireland where he managed to alienate both the native Irish and the Anglo-Norman lords who were carving out lands for themselves in England's Wild West, attempted to usurp his brother's throne, and spent a large part of his reign in opposition to his barons, it is difficult to see how history could have treated him otherwise. His succession was accepted in England and Normandy, but not in

Anjou, Maine or Touraine, where the local lords announced that they recognised John's nephew, Arthur, Duke of Brittany, as their overlord. As Arthur was twelve years old in 1199, he would be unlikely to interfere with the magnates' governance of their fiefs, and as the only legitimate grandson of Henry II in the male line he was inevitably going to find himself as a political football. He had been a ward of Richard I's, spent time at the French court, and paid homage to the French king and to John for Anjou, Maine and Brittany.

Then, in what seemed a shrewd and advantageous move, John put aside his first wife, Isabella of Gloucester, and married another Isabella, this time of Angoulême. The second Isabella had lands which lay between Normandy and Aquitaine that would be a useful addition to English possessions in France. However, there was a snag. The lady had previously been engaged to marry one Hugh of Lusignan, who objected to being deprived of his fiancée (and, presumably, the lands that she would bring with her) and appealed to King Philip of France. Philip, seizing the chance to discommode the English king, summoned John to appear before him and when John refused, in April 1200 he declared all John's continental fiefs forfeit.

In what was to be his only successful military campaign, John recovered the disputed territories and captured Arthur. The young duke disappeared into an English prison in Falaise where he may or may not have been mutilated on the orders of John, was transferred to Rouen and was never seen again. Legends varied from his having been killed by John personally and his body thrown in the Seine, to his having escaped and standing ready to reappear in Brittany when the time was ripe. That was John's last chance to retain his lands in France, for in 1204 the French king declared the Dukedom of Normandy forfeit and subsumed into the crown lands of France, the exception being the Channel Islands which remain British to this day. The tide of war now turned against the English and John lost all his French territories except Poitou, which was on the verge of surrender and only rescued by an expedition in 1206.

From then on John, his nickname now 'softsword' because of his military reverses, rather than 'lackland' from his lack of patrimony as a younger son, put all his energies into raising the wherewithal to recover his lost lands. This meant that he spent longer in England than any previous ruler since the conquest. It also meant increased and increasing taxation leading to more trouble with his barons, a breakdown in church-state relations – including a papal interdict on England and the excommunication of John personally, civil war, the signing of the Magna Carta, invasion and civil war again. When John died in 1216, his infant son Henry III inherited a kingdom divided by war, with rebellious barons in the north and the French dauphin Louis, touted by some as king rather than John, in the south. History has been unkind to Henry III, but with rather less cause than to his father. Fortunately, with the death of John, much of the impetus of the Barons' revolt was diffused, and in the south Louis was being seen as a foreign usurper rather than as an alternative king. There were sufficiently good men in the Midlands to back young Henry, and after the battle of Lincoln and a sea battle off Sandwich in 1217, the French claimant withdrew, helped on his way by a hefty bribe.

Like his father, Henry tried to rule as an autocrat, and like his father, he fell out with his magnates as a result. He had, however, the sense to realise that he could not rule alone, and by accepting his father's Magna Carta and (under pressure) dismissing the large number of grasping relations of his French wife who had flocked to England to make their fortune now that the Holy Land, re-conquered by the Muslims, was no longer an option, he was able to avoid being deposed. He too was no soldier, and in the Treaty of Paris in 1259 he gave up his claim to Normandy, Anjou and Maine. He retained only Aquitaine, but as a vassal of the French king to whom he had to pay homage. Despite all this, he did reign for fifty-six years and although the latter stages were marred by rebellion and civil war again, he did greatly improve the administrative machinery of government and promoted gothic architecture – his greatest artistic endeavour being the building of Westminster Abbey as a shrine to Edward the Confessor. He also left behind him a reasonably contented and more or less united kingdom, and an adult son who would begin to establish the military basis for a recovery of England's lost territories.

Historical revisionism is not confined to the wars of the twentieth century, and Edward I has come in for a fair bit of revisionism by modern writers. On the positive side, all agree that he was tall, athletic and handsome, a good soldier and genuinely in love with his wife, Eleanor of Castile, unusual when royal marriages were contracted for political and dynastic reasons regardless of the personal preferences of the individuals involved. To his detriment, he took up arms against his father during the civil wars with the barons, changed sides at least twice, and was accused of breaking solemn promises. Even after having returned to his allegiance and in command of the Royalist forces at the Battle of Evesham in 1265 he was accused of duplicity in the cornering of the rebel army and the death of their leader, Simon de Montfort, eighth Earl of Leicester. This latter refers to Edward's flying the banners of captured nobles either to give the impression that they had changed sides or to convince de Montfort that his rebel troops had the royalists surrounded. That would seem a perfectly legitimate *ruse de guerre*, although the behaviour of Roger Mortimer (another turncoat), who is alleged to have killed de Montfort, cut off his head and genitals and then sent the package to his own wife as a souvenir, would have been regarded as poor form even then. Mortimer also killed Sir Hugh Despenser at the same battle, a matter that would resurface half a century later.

Additionally, Edward had a vile temper, expelled the Jews from England in 1290 and profited thereby, and dealt with any opposition from the pope by fining his representatives in England. Most of the criticism of Edward relates to his time as the heir, and contemporary chroniclers are less strident when writing about his reign as king – but then denigrating a prince is one thing, opposing an anointed king quite another. The probable truth is that Edward was no more self-seeking and avaricious than any other great lord of the time, and less than many. In the twenty-first century West we regard personal integrity and unselfishness as vital in the conduct of our daily lives; most of us would put, or at least try to put, country and the common good before self, but this is not the norm in today's Third World, and it was not the norm in the medieval world. Then it would have seemed very odd indeed not to put the interests of one's own family before all else. We should beware of judging the past by the standards of the present.

One of Edward's first acts as king was to set up a commission to inquire into the very abuses that had precipitated civil war in his father's time, and he was assiduous in exposing and punishing corruption and misuse of office, provided it was not his own. As many of the magnates claimed rights and privileges on the grounds that they had held them 'since time immemorial', Edward defined this as prior to the accession of Richard I in 1189. Thus, any claim less than eighty-five years old had to be proved by hard evidence including documentary evidence and even then, was unlikely to be accepted. The administration of the realm was overhauled, and an unprecedented flurry of legislation dealt with such matters as land tenure, debt collection, feudal overlordship, ecclesiastical jurisdiction, landlord and tenant relations, grants to the church and family settlements. The criminal law too was brought up to date and the statute of Winchester of 1285 insisted upon the community's responsibility to lodge accusations of criminal conduct, ordered the roads to be improved and the undergrowth cut back to prevent ambushes by robbers, laid down what weapons were to be held by which classes to ensure the security of the kingdom, and made rape an offence for the king's justice rather than a local matter.

It is as a soldier and a castle builder that Edward is best remembered, and the early years of his reign saw the subjection of Wales and the virtual destruction of the Welsh nobility. Contemporary English propaganda, accusing the Welsh of sexual licence, robbery, brigandage, murder, every crime on the statute book and many not yet thought of may have been exaggerated. However, the Welsh princes had neither the administrative machinery nor the legal system to govern the country, and Edward's campaigns of 1276 to 1284 brought the rule of (English) law and good (or at least better) government to a backward people. Edward's announcement that the Welsh wanted a prince, and that he would give them one in his eldest son displayed to the people on a shield, is of course pure myth, although he did bestow the title of Prince of Wales on his heir. However brutal and of dubious legality Edward's subjugation of Wales may have been, modern Welsh nationalism has fed on a spurious legend of great warriors and an incorruptible native aristocracy that never existed. Then, in Edward's fifty-fourth year and the twenty-second of his reign came war with France in 1294, resulting from Philip IV's attempt to confiscate Aquitaine, simultaneous with a rising in Wales, and then a revolt in Scotland in 1297.

The preparations for the French war exposed the cracks in the feudal system of military service, which would linger on until the time of Edward III with a brief resurgence under Richard II. Under it, the king had the right to summon those who held lands from him to give him military service for a specific period, usually forty days, although it could be extended. These nobles with their retainers were supported by a militia of the common people who again could only be compelled to serve for a specific period. The Militia could not be mobilised during the planting season and had to be home again for the harvest. Wars were expensive: the troops had to be fed, housed, transported and in some cases paid and armed. There was no permanent commissariat and carts, horses, and the supplies that they carried had to be bought or hired. It was generally accepted that the king could not finance a campaign of any length from his own income, and taxes and customs dues were usually agreed by an assembly of the great men of the realm, now increasingly being referred to as the Parliament.

Initially, such taxes were freely voted. Then, as Edward needed more and more money and more and more men to reinforce his garrison in Aquitaine, he began to take shortcuts. Taxes were announced without consulting the parliament; the Dean of St Paul's is said to have died of apoplexy on hearing that the levy on the clergy was to be half of their assessed incomes. Merchants took grave exception to the compulsory purchase of wool at less than the market price, which the king then intended to sell abroad at a large profit. Royal agents who collected taxes and scoured the country for supplies and grain were said to be accepting bribes for exempting some men and keeping a portion of that collected for themselves. Many magnates summoned for military service refused to go. When Edward told the Earl of Norfolk that he had better go to Aquitaine or hang, he replied, correctly as it happened, that he would neither go nor hang. By the time Edward decided to take the field himself and sailed for Flanders in August 1297, the country was on the brink of civil war and there were those who feared a repetition of the Barons' Wars of Edward's father and grandfather. What saved him was a rising in Scotland.

The Scottish problem was not new, but up to the death of their king, Alexander III, in a riding accident in 1286, relations had been reasonably cordial. William the Lion of Scotland had done homage to Henry II, and it was generally accepted that the English king was the overlord of Scotland, albeit that he was not expected to interfere in its administration. Alexander left no male heirs, and his nearest relative was his six-year-old granddaughter, whose father was King Eric of Norway. Edward of England's plan, which might have saved much subsequent Anglo-Scottish enmity, was to marry the 'Maid of Norway' to his eldest son, Edward of Caernarvon, later Edward II, but when the maid died in the Orkneys on her way to Scotland in 1290 the inevitable rival claimants appeared from all corners of the country. Civil war was avoided by the Bishop of St Andrews asking Edward I to mediate between the starters, soon reduced to two: Robert Bruce (originally de Brus) and John Baliol, both descendants of Normans and both owning lands on both sides of the border, Baliol rather more than Bruce.

By a process that came to be known as the 'Great Cause', which appears at this distance to be reasonably fair and legally correct, Edward found in favour of Baliol who was duly crowned in 1292. At this point, Edward attempted to extend his influence into Scotland as he had in Wales. His overturning of decisions of the Scottish courts and attempts to enforce feudal military service from Scottish nobles, which Baliol did little to resist, led to a council of Scottish lords taking over the government from Baliol in 1295 and making a treaty of friendship with Philip IV of France. This could never be acceptable to England, with the threat of war on two fronts, and in a lightning and exceedingly brutal campaign in 1296, Edward destroyed the Scottish armies and accepted the unconditional surrender of the Scottish leaders including Baliol. Had Edward reinstalled Baliol and backed off from insisting on what he saw as his feudal rights all might have been well. However, by imposing English rule under a viceroy, Earl Warenne, with English governors in each district and English prelates being appointed to vacant Scottish livings, and by adding insult to defeat by removing the Stone of Scone,* on which Scottish kings were crowned, to England, revolt was inevitable. It duly broke out in 1297, as Edward arrived in Flanders to intervene personally in the war against the French.

Almost immediately all the resentment that had been building up in England against Edward for his unjust methods of financing the French campaign dissipated. War abroad against the French was one thing, but revolt by what most English lords saw as English subjects was quite another. Robert Bruce, previously a loyal subject of Edward but dismayed by the failure to grant the throne to him, was easily dealt with by Warenne, but then a massacre of an overconfident English army at Stirling Bridge in an ambush skilfully conducted by William Wallace in September 1297 outraged and frightened the English government. Edward came to terms with Philip IV, returned from Flanders, and at the Battle of Falkirk in July 1298 he slaughtered Wallace's Scottish army. It was the bloodiest battle on British soil until Towton in 1461 but it was not decisive. Although the Scots would not for a long time risk meeting an English army in the open field, their hit and run tactics would drag the conflict on until 1304, when the majority of the Scottish leaders came to terms with Edward.

Wallace himself was tried as a traitor and suffered the prescribed punishment of being hanged until nearly dead, then being disembowelled and castrated, and his intestines and genitalia

---

* Placed under the coronation chair in Westminster Abbey it has been part of the coronation of every English and British monarch since. It was returned to Scotland in 1996 but was brought back to London for the coronation of Charles III.

being burnt in front of him before he was finally decapitated. His body was then divided into four parts, a quarter to be exhibited in different cities, while the head was placed on a pike above Tower Bridge. This was only a temporary respite, however. Robert Bruce, who had initially revolted in 1297 but then changed sides and supported Edward's subsequent campaigning, led another rising in 1306 and, having eliminated another claimant to the throne by murdering him, had himself crowned as king. More battles followed, and when Edward I died on his way to Scotland in 1307, exhorting his son on his deathbed to continue his conquest of the northern kingdom, the horrendous costs of warfare were revealed in the crown's debts of £200,000 or around £200 million today.

This book is not a sociological treatise, and this author has no intention of exploring why so often in history the sons of great men turn out to be craven weaklings but suffice it to say that if Edward I has been subject to historical revisionism, then none is necessary for his son. Edward II was every bit as unpleasant and incompetent as the chroniclers claim. Although he inherited his father's commanding height and good looks and was a competent horseman, he had little interest in the other knightly virtues and corrupted the system of royal patronage. This latter depended for its success on the wide and reasonably fair distribution of land, offices and titles, thus retaining the loyalty of those who mattered, but Edward neglected the magnates who expected to be preferred and instead lavished favours and lands on his successive catamites. Homosexuality was not then a civil crime, but it was a sin in the eyes of the church – it was equated with heresy – and generally regarded with horror by the laity.

Edward's proclivities might have been tolerated if he had kept them as private as it was possible to be in a medieval court, but this he was unable to do. Some modern scholarship has suggested that Edward's relationships were not sexual but actually a form of blood brotherhood and point to the fact that open accusations of homosexuality against Edward were not made until after his death (hardly surprising), but rather only hinted at. That Edward and both his favourites were married and produced children is no defence: all three had to produce heirs and it is not at all uncommon for homosexuals to engage in occasional normal relationships. While at the time it was not unusual for men to share a bed without any impropriety (indeed soldiers in British army barrack rooms were required to sleep two or three to a bed until well into the nineteenth century) to choose to sleep with a man rather than with one's wife on the night of one's coronation, as Edward did, would seem to be conclusive. That the magnates had their doubts about Edward II from a very early stage is evidenced by their insertion of a new clause in the coronation oath, whereby Edward swore to uphold 'the laws and customs of the realm'.

Edward's first favourite, who had been part of his household since he was Prince of Wales, was Piers Gaveston, a Gascon knight and son of a loyal servant and soldier of Edward I. Knighted by Edward I and then advanced to the earldom of Cornwall (a title normally reserved for princes of the blood royal) by Edward II, Gaveston was intelligent, good looking, a competent administrator and excelled at the knightly pastimes of hunting and jousting. All might have been well if he could only have restrained his wit and avoided poking fun at the great men of the kingdom. Had he deferred to the nobility and worked at showing them that he was no threat (and he appears to have had no political ambitions) he might well occupy but a brief footnote in history, but as it was, he could not resist teasing the magnates to whom he gave offensive and often apt nicknames, of which he made no secret. Thus, the amply proportioned Earl of Lincoln was 'burst belly', the Earl of Pembroke 'Joseph the Jew', the Earl of Lancaster, the king's cousin, the richest man in the kingdom and the proprietor of a large private army, was 'the fiddler' and the Earl of Warwick, who would ultimately be responsible for Gaveston's premature demise, 'the black dog of Arden'. Not only did Gaveston make no secret of his deriding of the great men, but he also publicly humiliated them by beating them in jousts and took a prominent role in the coronation that should have been filled by men of far higher status. Gaveston married the king's niece, a union to which his birth did not entitle him, and when Edward went to France to collect his own bride, he left Gaveston as regent.

By his behaviour, and by his position as the king's principal adviser, Gaveston was bound to make dangerous enemies: he was exiled once by Edward I and twice by Edward II under pressure from the magnates who threatened civil war if the favourite did not go. Then, in 1312, Gaveston's return from exile for the third time did spark baronial revolt. He eventually fell into the hands of his enemies, principally the Earl of Warwick, and after a trial which was probably illegal, he was condemned to death and beheaded near Kenilworth on land belonging to the Earl of Lancaster. As was the norm at the time, no one actually blamed the king for all the injustices and inefficiencies of his reign, but rather his evil councillor – Gaveston – and Edward was then in no position to do anything about what he saw as the murder of his beloved Pierot (his pet name for Gaveston). Revenge was to come later.

Despite the removal of Gaveston, by 1314 baronial opposition to Edward's rule, or misrule, was growing. Having ignored his father's dying wish that he should complete the conquest of Scotland, Edward II had abandoned that nation to civil war and returned south. Now, hoping to restore the political situation at home through a successful war in Scotland, Edward summoned the earls to report for military service. The Earl of Lancaster and a number of his supporters refused, on the grounds that Parliament had not approved the finances for the expedition, which was therefore illegal. Edward went ahead anyway, and the result was a disaster when his army of around 10,000 was decisively defeated by a much smaller Scottish army commanded by Robert Bruce at Bannockburn in June 1314. Edward fled the field (to be fair he wanted to stand and fight but his minders would not have it) and his army collapsed with perhaps a third becoming casualties. Disaster although it undoubtedly was for Edward, the battle was the trigger for a root and branch reform of the English military system which would contribute much to the superiority of English arms in the Hundred Years War to come.

As the Scottish war dragged on without any prospect of a successful end, Edward's position weakened further. Scottish raids into northern England were increasingly ambitious, Berwick on Tweed* was under siege yet again, and there was revolt in Wales. To make matters worse, new favourites began increasingly to engage Edward's attention and to receive favours from him. The Despensers, father and son, both named Hugh, were rather better bred than Gaveston had been, but were actually more of a threat, being even more avaricious than the previous royal pet, in the case of Hugh the Younger with political ambitions and the ability to pursue them. There is less evidence for a homosexual relationship between Edward and Hugh the Younger than there was for the Gaveston affair. However, in the behaviour of the king towards him there can be little doubt that the friendship was a lot more than just the comradeship of men both in their thirties. The Despenser methods of increasing their holdings of land varied from blackmail, intimidation of the courts, the threat and sometimes use of force, and outright theft. In this, they particularly upset the Marcher Lords who found estates in Wales and on the border that should have gone to them being acquired by the Despensers, while early on Hugh the Younger upset the Earl of Lancaster when he was granted a potentially lucrative wardship which Lancaster had attempted to obtain for himself.

Antagonism towards the Despensers exploded in 1321 when the Marcher Lords, aided by Lancaster, attacked Despenser lands and properties. In Parliament in London, the lords laid the usual charges against them: removal of competent officials by the Despensers and their replacement by corrupt ones; refusing access to the king unless one of them was present; misappropriating properties and generally giving the king bad advice. Edward, backed into a corner and faced with the united opposition of so many had little choice but to agree to Parliament's demands and the Despensers were duly exiled.

Now began Edward's only successful military campaign of his entire reign. Lancaster, for all his titles and riches, was neither a

---

* Described by Robbie Burns as 'A bridge without a middle arch, a church without a steeple, a midden heap in every street, and damned conceited people'; Berwick changed hands between England and Scotland thirteen times between the eleventh and fifteenth centuries.

natural leader, a competent general nor politically astute: he was indecisive, and he too had his enemies. Once away from the London Parliament Edward recalled the Despensers, besieged and took Leeds Castle in Kent, executed the commander and his garrison and marched north. Lancaster too moved north, possibly to seek sanctuary with the Scots, and on 16 March 1322 found his way barred by a royalist army at Boroughbridge, which held the only bridge over the River Ure. Unable to force the bridge, the Earl of Hereford being killed in the attempt, and prevented by royalist archers from crossing at a nearby ford – lessons that would also be relevant to the great war that was to come – Lancaster's army melted away and the Earl himself surrendered the next day. Tried as a traitor at Pontefract, the Earl of Lancaster could have expected to have been pardoned with a fine or exiled at worst in deference to his royal blood (he was a grandson of Henry III) but now it was payback time for Gaveston, and the only concession to Lancaster was that he was beheaded rather than hanged, drawn and quartered.

Despite Lancaster's unpleasant traits, such was the unpopularity of the king and the Despensers that a cult rapidly grew up and royal guards had to be posted over Lancaster's tomb to prevent miracle seekers from approaching it. Having dealt with Lancaster Edward's revenge on the other rebels was bloody: eleven barons and fifteen knights were drawn, hanged, and quartered, four Kentish knights were drawn and hanged, but not quartered, in Canterbury and another in London, while seventy-two knights were imprisoned. From now until 1326, the Despenser power, wealth and influence increased: their mistake, and the cause of their ultimate downfall, was in attracting the opposition of the queen.

Chapter Two – Stating the Claim

For 391 years, ever since Hugh Capet, a direct descendant of Charlemagne, acquired the French throne by election, the Capets had ruled France. On 29 November 1314 Philip IV, the thirteenth Capetian king, died leaving three sons. All three reigned after him. Louis X reigned from 1314 to 1316. He was the first to build indoor tennis courts and died of what may have been pleurisy after drinking a prodigious amount of cooled wine on completion of a particularly vigorous game.* He left an infant son born a few days before he died, who was technically king as John I before he too died five days later. He was succeeded by Louis' brother, Philip, who died in 1322, probably of dysentery, without leaving a legitimate son. Philip V was followed by the third brother, Charles IV. Charles died suddenly in 1328, the cause unknown to us. His wife was pregnant when he died and if the issue had been a son, then the succession would have been assured, but the child was a daughter. As French custom forbade the throne passing to a woman, with the death of Charles the Capetian dynasty came to an end.

While Philip IV had three sons, he also had a daughter, Isabella, born in 1295. Isabella has, somewhat unfairly, gone down in English history as the 'she wolf of France' but she was described as being very beautiful (her brothers and father were also regarded as very handsome), intelligent and, unusual for a girl at that time, well educated. She was married to Edward of Carnarvon, later Edward II, at Boulogne in 1307 when she was aged twelve and he twenty-three. At that time the church permitted sexual intercourse from the age of twelve provided the girl had passed puberty, and from the contemporary descriptions of her, Isabella seems to have done so. It is true that she has been described as a notorious adulteress, a rebel against her husband and complicit in his murder. Her discovery of an adulterous relationship by the wives of two of her brothers with the connivance of the wife of a third

---

* Although there were persistent rumours that he had been poisoned.

and her eventual reporting of it to her father, Philip IV, in full knowledge of what the result might be, has been cited as evidence of a hard-heartedness in her character. However, it is far more likely that she knew what her punishment might be if she concealed such knowledge.

Margarite of Burgundy was the wife of Louis, later Louis X, and Blanche of Hungary was married to Charles, later Charles IV. Both young ladies, aided and abetted by Jeanne of Burgundy, wife of Philip, later Philip V, were carrying on with two knights of the French court, the brothers Philip and Gautier d'Aulnay. On the information laid by Isabella, all five were arrested and the brothers tortured until they admitted to adultery – a particularly serious offence as it could call the whole royal succession into question. The wretched knights were publicly castrated with their organs thrown to the hounds, then flayed until almost dead and finally decapitated. Margarite and Blanche were sentenced to life imprisonment in Chateau Gaillard, while Jeanne was put under house arrest.

Withal, Isabella did have a great deal to put up with. Her husband obviously preferred his male lovers to her, and it was particularly galling that jewellery from her father meant for her was given to Gaveston. Despite his proclivities, Edward did manage to rise to the occasion and give his wife four children: Edward (the future Edward III) born in 1312, John in 1316, Eleanor in 1318, and Joan in 1321. Indeed, for the first years of their marriage, she supported her husband against his barons, and in disagreements with her own father and brothers, kings of France. Despite Gaveston's relationship with her husband, Isabella seems to have got on reasonably well with him, or at least to have tolerated him, during the five years that she knew him. But when he was killed in June 1312, to be replaced in her husband's favours by the Despensers, matters took a more sinister turn. Unlike Gaveston, who was a nuisance but not a threat, the Despensers, father and son, were a threat both to the landed nobility and to the Queen herself. The Despensers began to move against her, suspecting that she was in contact with their enemies, as she probably was. They persuaded the king to resume her property on the grounds that they should not, as an independent source of funds, be left in her hands as Anglo-French relations worsened. It was then that Isabella's attitudes began to change. She did retain the confidence of the king in political matters, for when war over Aquitaine broke out again in 1324, it was Isabella, with the approval of the over-confident Despensers, who was sent to France to mediate with her brother, Charles IV. Charles had succeeded his brother Philip V in 1322, and while he was undoubtedly supportive of Isabella as his sister, he also saw her as a possible pawn which could be manipulated to discommode the English king.

The queen was well aware of the enmity of the Despensers but was clever enough to bid an ostensibly amiable farewell to Hugh the Younger on leaving Dover for France, and to send him friendly letters from Paris. In her discussions with her brother Charles, Isabella seems genuinely to have wanted a solution to the issues between England and France that would benefit her adopted country and her husband its king, while still being acceptable to the French. A major disagreement that would arise over and over again was the exact status of the English holdings in France, particularly Aquitaine. Were they held in absolute possession by the King of England, or did he hold them by leave of the King of France? If the latter, did he hold them in simple homage, which acknowledged that the lands were controlled by England but held from the King of France, or liege homage, which carried with it a feudal obligation of service to that French king? Liege homage was something that would never be acceptable to any English monarch, or indeed to any Englishman. At one stage Edward was prepared to come and pay simple homage in person, but then the Despensers, fearful for their own position if the king was out of the country, persuaded him not to go. It was agreed, probably at Isabella's instigation, that Edward would grant his eldest son all his titles and lands in France, and that the son, rather than the father, would go to France to pay homage. Whether this was a genuine attempt by Isabella to resolve the conflict, or whether it was a ploy to obtain control of the heir to the throne is still the subject of debate – though it was probably a bit of both. In any event, Isabella and Edward, Prince of Wales, who was not quite thirteen, set sail from Dover with their entourage, including two bishops and a number of knights, on 12 September 1325 and Edward paid homage to his uncle Charles at Vincennes on 24 September.

With a truce brokered and the English lands safe in the hands of the heir, there was now no need for Isabella and her son to remain in France and the king expected their return. At first, this took the form of enquiries as to their travel arrangements, with the queen giving various reasons why she should stay a little longer, but as the king's enquiries became demands that she and his son should return, she made it clear that she would not set foot in England until the Despensers were exiled, as she feared for her safety if she returned. In the meantime, she began to become a focus for various disenchanted Englishmen and exiled nobles in France, something that was duly reported back to the king by emissaries sent to escort her back, and by members of her own household whom she returned to England when the king stopped her allowance. The King of France, her brother, was initially happy to pay Isabella's bills, but then she became embroiled in scandal, the other party being Roger Mortimer.

Roger Mortimer was born in 1287, into a family that was already enormously rich with lands in the Welsh Marches and mid-Wales, southern England, the Midlands, and Ireland, but when his father died in 1304 and he was seventeen, his wardship was given by Edward I to his son who gave it to Piers Gaveston. A wardship was immensely lucrative as all the income from the ward's estates was controlled by the guardian (and could be diverted to his own purposes) until the ward reached his majority, then twenty-one. The guardian also controlled his ward's marriage, and in 1306 Roger paid Gaveston 2,500 Marks (equivalent to £17,000) to claim his estates and income for the rest of his minority. As his minority had only two years to run, the payment indicates how valuable the estates were. At first Roger's life was like that of any other sprig of the nobility: knighted by the ageing Edward I in the same year as he reclaimed his estates and in the same batch as the Prince of Wales, later Edward II, he played an official role in the latter's coronation, served in Aquitaine, took part in the suppression of revolt in Wales, and served two terms as Justiciar of Ireland where he was as successful as any English peacemaker could be in that lawless land.

From 1320, towards the end of his second tour in Ireland, Roger became increasingly part of the opposition to the Despensers as they extended their holdings in Wales to what the Marcher Lords, which included him, saw as their detriment. In any case, it was said that Hugh Despenser the Younger was determined, in the manner of a Pathan blood feud, to wreak vengeance on Roger Mortimer for the death of Hugh's grandfather at the hands of Roger's grandfather at the battle of Evesham in 1265. As we have seen, the success of the baronial opposition to the Despensers in 1321 was short-lived. The battle of Boroughbridge on 16 March 1322 ended the civil war but before that Roger Mortimer and his uncle, Roger Mortimer of Chirk, had already surrendered to the king at Shrewsbury on 23 January. They were sentenced to death but spared the terrible fate of so many of their fellow rebels when the sentence was commuted to life imprisonment in the Tower of London.

On 1 August 1323 in a Buchanesque adventure involving conniving jailers and drugged sentries, Roger Mortimer escaped from the Tower, obtained a boat in which he rowed across the Thames, stole or was given a horse, rode to Dover, found a ship to cross the Channel to France and was welcomed at the court of Charles IV, then at loggerheads with Edward II over the usual vexed question of Aquitaine. Mortimer now joined the band of expatriate Englishmen clustered around the French court or at that of the Count of Hainault, part of modern Belgium, and also in opposition to Edward II's England, while his uncle stayed in the Tower, his lands forfeited, and died there aged seventy in 1326.

Roger Mortimer did not stay long in Paris and spent the next year or so in Hainault trying to raise troops and money to mount an invasion of England encouraged by the Count and by disaffected elements in England who vowed they would rise if an invasion to remove the Despensers were to happen. Isabella probably first met Mortimer at the funeral of the old Count of

Valois, when he came to Paris in the entourage of the Countess of Hainault. As both he and Isabella were united in hatred and fear of the Despensers, it was natural that they should meet, and that Roger should confer with the English opposition now coalescing around the queen.

Remarkably quickly their relationship became more than a political alliance and by at least early 1326 it was generally assumed that they were sleeping together. While it was considered normal for married men to have mistresses (and Mortimer had been separated from his own wife for three years) for a lady to play away was regarded as a heinous crime, and for a queen to do so was treason of the worst sort. One can only assume that Isabella knew this perfectly well but that she was motivated by years of sexual frustration and resentment of her husband's actions towards her and his predilection for unsavoury favourites. She was a mature beauty of thirty-one and the thirty-nine years old Mortimer was, after all, everything King Edward was not: sexually normal, decisive, outgoing, audacious, and sharing her interest in culture and the arts. We today might not blame either of them but at the time both were playing a dangerous game.

Once the news of their relationship reached England – and it did so remarkably quickly – Edward redoubled his efforts to force his eldest son[*] to return to his allegiance, even if the boy's mother would not. Letters were sent to the King of France, to the Pope, to his son and to anyone else who might listen, but to no avail. Rumours of invasion were rife and throughout the summer Edward issued commissions of array calling up troops, sequestered ships to watch the maritime approaches, and ordered coastal defences to be put in order. He seized Isabella's remaining lands and confiscated her funds lodged in the Tower, attempted to arrest Mortimer's mother (she was tipped off and went into hiding), and locked up anyone else who might be sympathetic to the queen or who might oppose the Despensers and whom he could

---

[*] He did have a second son, John, but while he might have wished that he could replace Edward as heir presumptive with John, the church and the (unwritten) constitution would never have countenanced it.

lay hands on. Eventually, having failed to persuade Charles IV to cooperate, Edward declared war on France in July 1326.

At last Edward's appeals to the Pope in Avignon bore fruit: John XXII had hoped to keep the peace between England and France and had sent nuncios to try to mediate between Isabella and her husband, but he could not condone adultery and he wrote to Charles IV to tell him so. Charles, no doubt mindful of what had happened to his ex-wife Blanche and her illicit lover, agreed to expel Isabella and Mortimer, but it would seem to have been done in a gentlemanly way. The couple were given lots of notice and Isabella was allowed to take all her possessions and funds provided by Charles with her. She now accepted, if she had not done so before, that it was not just the Despensers that were her enemies, but her husband the king of England as well. Since his escape from the Tower Mortimer had always hoped to overthrow Edward II and now Isabella became part of the plan too – and it was she who possessed the strongest card, the king's son, Edward, Prince of Wales. After a diversion to Isabella's county of Ponthieu to raise funds, she and Mortimer were welcomed in Hainault in August.

Now the plan to invade England and depose Edward II in favour of his son began to be put into action. Young Edward was betrothed to the eighteen year old Philippa, daughter of the Count of Hainault, who brought with her a dowry of men, money and ships to be placed at Isabella's disposal immediately. These joined with troops raised by Mortimer and gathered at the assembly port of Dordrecht, southeast of Rotterdam. There were no French troops involved: not only was Charles IV fully engaged in Aquitaine but Isabella and Mortimer both knew that the fastest way to make their support in England evaporate overnight would be for a single French soldier to land on English shores. Edward II was well aware of what was being planned and on 2 September he ordered the Earl of Norfolk to raise 2,000 troops from East Anglia to defend the port of Orwell in Suffolk. Whether Edward's intelligence service, such as it was, had discovered that port to be the intended landing area, or whether he concluded that an invasion mounted from the port of Dordrecht would probably make for Orwell we do not know. In any event the troops were never raised and the Earl, the king's half-brother, went over to Isabella. Edward does not seem to have checked whether his orders were being obeyed.

At Dordrecht, Isabella, Mortimer and her army embarked on ninety-five ships, and put to sea on 22 September 1326. The army was a mix of Flemish, German, and Bohemian soldiers, mainly mercenaries but with some unpaid volunteers hopeful of making their fortunes, and a gaggle of English exiles and emissaries sent by Edward II who had then sided with Isabella and stayed abroad. Accounts as to their numbers vary depending upon which chronicle one relies upon but given the capacity of the ships of the time and the need to transport horses and equipment, the force was probably around 1,500 strong. It was a tiny army with which to mount an invasion, even by medieval standards, but Isabella had good reason to expect indigenous support once she landed, and she and Mortimer had probably concluded a secret treaty with the Scots (which was to come back and haunt them later) to ensure that Robert Bruce, styled King Robert I, did not invade northern England while Isabella was dealing with Edward II. In the event, the campaign was even easier than Isabella and Mortimer could have hoped. After two days of being tossed about in a storm, the invasion force landed somewhere near the mouth of the River Orwell on 24 September, unopposed by the king's ships which were either not in the vicinity or had mutinied against the Despensers.

Most of the nobility had now accepted that the influence of the Despensers was intolerable and that the king would not reform. The time had finally come to remove this ineffective and capricious monarch and replace him with his son. To most, the queen was seen as a tragic figure, more sinned against than sinning, and public opinion soon swung in her favour as more and more of the barons and their troops rallied to her. Edward's support melted away and he and the Despensers and what adherents they still had fled to Wales, where they no doubt hoped for support from the Despensers' tenants there. It was not to be, and when the garrison of Bristol surrendered on 26 October, Hugh the Elder was taken, tried for numerous offences and executed the following day, with his head sent to Winchester for public exhibition.

On 16 November 1326, the king and the younger Despenser were captured at Llantrisant, near Caerphilly. Appropriately enough their captor was Henry of Lancaster, brother of Thomas who had been executed after Boroughbridge in 1322. Hugh Despenser was taken to Hereford, condemned to death as a traitor, a heretic and a sodomite, hung from fifty feet high gallows, cut down while still alive, castrated, disembowelled, and finally beheaded. The king was sent to Kenilworth and on 20 January 1327 was persuaded to abdicate in favour of his eldest son, who was duly crowned as Edward III on 1 February.

The deposed Edward was now transferred to Berkeley Castle, and there were a number of plots to rescue him, some real, many more imagined. Then, during a parliamentary session at Lincoln, it was announced that Edward had died on 21 September 1327. Whether or not he did die, and if so the cause and manner of it, has intrigued historians ever since. At the time it was stated to be from 'natural causes', but as Edward was only 43 at the time of his death this seems unlikely. A lurid account written thirty years later, but probably circulating orally shortly after the king's death, and sniggered over by schoolboys ever since, says that he was killed by having a red hot poker or spit shoved up his bottom. This too seems unlikely and is more probably intended as a cautionary tale against homosexuality (Edward was reckoned by contemporaries to be the buggeree in his relationships). The body of a dead king would have to be put on public display to avoid claims that he had been spirited away and was in hiding (and such tales of Edward II did arise), and charred flesh in the nether regions would surely be noticed during the removal of organs as part of the embalming process. It seems much more likely that the wretched Edward was smothered, a means of despatch which leaves no marks on the body. The body was displayed in Gloucester from 22 October and buried there in the presence of Isabella and the new king shortly afterwards. On 30 January 1328, Edward married Philippa. It was to be a genuinely happy marriage, despite Edward's later womanising, but at this early stage, there was to be little time for domestic bliss, for the new regime had problems enough.

The first problem facing the new regime in England, and the one most in need of a conclusion, was the ever-present running sore of the Scots. Robert Bruce had adhered to his promise not to raid England during Isabella's invasion and subsequent campaign. But now with the deposition of Edward II, his assurances no longer held, and bands of ferocious Scots were raiding the northern English counties. It seemed that a short and successful war would cement the popularity of the new dynasty and Edward, his mother and Mortimer began to gather an army in York. The assembly was marred by an argument between English archers and the servants of Flemish men at arms sent from Hainault. Fuelled by the endemic English dislike of foreigners, the argument turned to a fight and then to a slaughter with the archers shooting indiscriminately at anyone who appeared alien. When order was restored, there were 300 dead in the streets of York, mainly Hainaulters. It was perhaps an omen for the campaign which began with the English army floundering about over an inhospitable terrain where it mostly poured with rain, trying to find the Scots who had no intention of fighting an open battle, and ended with an exhausted English army withdrawing. Edward was furious and was said to have wept in frustration.

Now it was increasingly clear to Isabella and to Mortimer that this was an unwinnable war. Even in the glory days of Edward I's Scottish wars, the Scots had always eventually returned to the fray, and the incessant border raids and the consequent punitive expeditions were a drain on resources and funds that England could ill afford. English emissaries began to negotiate with the Scots and the result was the Treaty of Northampton, ratified by Edward III in May 1328. The treaty acknowledged Scottish independence and the position of Robert Bruce as king and gave up English overlordship of Scotland (claimed by English kings ever since the Conquest). England agreed to return various relics including the 'black rood' (a sliver of wood that the Scots believed was from the cross on which Christ was crucified), the 'ragman' (a parchment submitting to Edward I with the seals of most of the great men of Scotland affixed to it) and the Stone of Scone. It was agreed that Robert Bruce's four year old son, David, would marry Isabella's seven year old daughter, Joan. In return Robert Bruce was to pay a £20,000 indemnity for Scottish raids into England and to agree to support England against any enemy except the French. As there was no other likely enemy, this was a rather hollow promise. In hindsight the treaty was a piece of pragmatic common sense. If Scotland could not be brought to heel, then give them what they want in exchange for perpetual peace and join the two crowns by a marriage deal. Additionally, security in the north would mean that Edward could pursue a French war without constantly having to look over his shoulder.

Unfortunately, that was not how it was seen in England. 'The Shameful Peace' had given away a princess, acknowledged the success of treason, given up the English crown's hereditary privileges over Scotland and, crucially, had not addressed the rights of English lords who held lands in Scotland. As by the treaty they now had no rights there, these lords styled themselves the 'Disinherited'. The young Edward made no secret of the fact that he disapproved of the treaty, saying that it was all his mother's and Mortimer's doing, and that he frowned on the wedding of his sister and would not attend the ceremony. No doubt some of this was a swift adoption of sloping shoulders once he realised the extent of public opinion, and in any case, the London mob prevented the Abbot of Westminster from releasing the Stone of Scone. Almost overnight Isabella's popularity began to wane, and by extension that of Mortimer.

Hot on the heels of the conclusion of the Scottish war came the news of the death of Charles IV of France, and so his sister Isabella was swift to send emissaries to Paris to register her claim. The stage was set for the Hundred Years War, for the other claimant was the thirty-five year old Philip of Valois, Count of Anjou and Maine. He was the son of Charles of Valois, who was a brother of Philip IV 'The Fair'. Philip's claim was based on being the nephew of one king (Philip IV) and the cousin of three others (Louis X, John I, Philip V, and the late departed Charles IV), whereas Edward III's mother Isabella was the daughter of a king and the sister of three others. Thus, if the succession was to be decided by consanguinity, Isabella's claim was the stronger. The so-called Salic Law, supposedly part of the legal code of the ancient Merovingian Franks and which forbade descent through the female line, was not trotted out and relied upon until very much later, but it is true that there had never been a queen regnant of France. When the question had last arisen, in 1316, the girl's guardian had conveniently withdrawn her claim. Isabella's emissaries, Bishops Orleton and Northburgh, argued that there was no legal justification for excluding her and pointed out that the greatest duchies (such as Aquitaine) could be, and had been, inherited by females, and that other kingdoms – Hungary, Bohemia – had been ruled by females of cadet branches of the Capets. Furthermore, they argued, even if there was justification for excluding a woman this argument could not be extended to Isabella's son who was the closest male descendant of Philip IV and the closest male relative to the late King Charles. This was a sensible shift – claiming the throne for Edward rather than for his mother – for if the latter's claim was pressed, then in logic, her dead brother's daughters would also have a claim.

Whatever the legal arguments might be the French were determined not to have Isabella on their throne, nor to accept her fifteen year old son. Not only was Edward of England a foreigner (although he would not have considered himself such) but he was a mere boy and would simply be the figurehead for his mother and her very dubious (in French eyes) lover, Mortimer. Philip of Valois, on the other hand, was a vigorous adult and a member of one of the greatest families of France, and Isabella's representatives found little support for her claim. Philip of Valois was proclaimed King of France as Philip VI, and the Burgomaster of Bruges, who was unwise enough to voice his countrymen's support for Edward, was mutilated and hanged as a warning to others.

Isabella would never relinquish her and her son's claim to the throne of France, but for the moment there was very little she could do about it. When the new King of France demanded homage for Aquitaine and Ponthieu on pain of invading Aquitaine, Isabella's first reaction was to refuse, but when Philip began to seize the incomes of the wine trade Edward had no option but to cross to France in 1329 and pay homage in Amiens cathedral. Technically the act of homage would negate any claim to the French throne, but later it was argued that Edward had not removed his spurs, nor his crown, nor had he knelt and so the act was meaningless. In any case, he had not done it freely but in the face of force majeure. For the moment, however, neither Edward nor his mother were in any position to press his claim.

The rule of Isabella and Mortimer, at first greeted with acclaim as a relief from the unstable and increasingly oppressive reign of Edward II, was now beginning to be viewed with as much dread as Edward's and the Despensers' had been. It was obvious to all that Isabella controlled the young king, and Mortimer controlled Isabella. Mortimer acquired more land and riches and, by having himself created Earl of March, set himself above all other Marcher lords in precedence. As Isabella was intelligent enough to realise the opposition that such tyrannical behaviour had aroused during her late husband's reign, one can only suppose that she was in such thrall to Mortimer that she could not or would not curb his ambitions. When rumours began to circulate about her being pregnant by Mortimer, which if true (almost certainly not) was a scandal of enormous proportions, the young king had had enough of being controlled by Mortimer through his mother. On 15 June 1330 with the court at Woodstock, Queen Philippa gave birth to a son, Edward of Woodstock, the future Black Prince. That same summer, the court moved to Nottingham, and Mortimer issued writs for a meeting of the great council of the realm, with nobles being warned that staying away would attract heavy penalties.

Mortimer was well aware that he was unpopular, that the young friends of the king were urging him to assert his authority, and that with the king approaching his majority and with a healthy heir-apparent, the rule of Isabella and Mortimer was under threat unless they managed somehow to persuade or intimidate the council into extending it. On the evening of 19 October 1330, the magnates left the castle at the conclusion of the day's business and the gates were duly locked. Later a group of the king's supporters led by the governor of the castle, whose soldiers had been replaced by Mortimer's men, entered the castle by way of a tunnel that ran from the town into the castle keep. There they were met by the king and taken to Isabella and Mortimer's apartments. The king remained outside while his party burst in to find Mortimer in discussion with the chancellor, the Bishop of Lincoln. In the ensuing scuffle, two of Mortimer's bodyguards were killed, and Mortimer and the bishop were seized and dragged out through the tunnel. The next morning, Mortimer's associates were arrested, and the party was taken to the Tower, while the king called a parliament to meet at Westminster and announced that henceforth he would rule fairly and with the advice of the great men of the kingdom. He was just eighteen years of age.

In November 1330, parliament duly met in London. Mortimer was condemned unheard and sentenced to death along with two of his most notorious adherents. On 29 November he was drawn to Tyburn on a hurdle and hanged, as were his two collaborators on Christmas Eve. All three were spared the more exotic refinements of a traitor's execution and were permitted burial. Edward had taken pains to ensure that no mention of his mother was made in the trials, and she was merely pensioned off to live in some style at Castle Rising.

Edward now had to rectify the oppression of his father's reign and that of Mortimer and Isabella. Many of the officials of the two previous regimes were given a short period in the wilderness but then re-employed if they were able administrators, which many of them were. All land grants made (by him in name, but by Isabella and Mortimer in reality) since his accession were cancelled, and laws forbidding duels, unofficial tournaments, and the bearing of arms in parliament were strengthened. Outside the immediate control of the king and his government, England was a lawless land: brigandage was rife, justices, whether those of Edward II or Mortimer, were corrupt, and the exhibition of various body parts of notable persons acted as a reminder of the dangers of choosing the wrong side in what had been a violently fluctuating political landscape. Great lords maintained private armies and often behaved very much as they liked, while always having to jockey for position depending upon whose star was in the ascendant at any particular time. Whether Edward III saw war abroad as being a way to channel English aggression to the common good, or whether he was mainly concerned with what he saw as his rightful inheritance through his mother, is irrelevant – it was probably a bit of both – but in any event, it is clear that from very early on he was intending to take on the French king. Before he could do that, however, he had to ensure that his back door was secure and that if he took an army to France he was not going to be invaded by the Scots. Any risk of French assistance to the Scots was reduced by a promise by Edward that in due course he would embark on a crusade with Philip.

It took Edward four campaigns to be sure that Scotland was safe, but he had to maintain the fiction that the Scots were the aggressors, otherwise by the treaty of Northampton he would have to return the £20,000 reparations paid by the Scots – actually a loan to them from the Pope and a sum long since spent by Isabella. Initially, he hid behind the 'Disinherited', those holders of lands north of the border who had lost out in the Northampton settlement. They, led by Edward Baliol, son of the deposed king John Baliol, raised an army and landed in Scotland. Openly Edward III condemned the move, refused the Disinherited passage over English territory and confiscated the estates of their supporters in England (quietly returning them a few months later). Initially, with Scotland divided and ruled by a regency for the six year old king, David Bruce, the Disinherited made startling progress. Although he had by no means conquered all of Scotland, Edward Baliol was nevertheless crowned at Scone in September 1332 and promised to pay homage to Edward III for the whole country. The English pretence of non-intervention began to unravel with the arrival of King David and his court as refugees in France. However, with the Pope anxious to prevent the two major Christian powers from going to war and having granted the French king a tax on the clergy to fund a projected crusade, a peace of sorts was maintained save for a few insignificant French raids on the Channel Islands and a handful of French horsemen landed in Scotland.

Then, in 1333, there was a resurgence of the Bruce faction who captured Berwick and embarked on the age-old Scottish sport of raiding into England. Edward was able to claim that it was the Scots who had broken the treaty and not he, and in went an English army that soundly trounced the Scots at Halidon Hill. Further expeditions followed in 1334, 1335 and 1336 until Edward was able to penetrate to the farthest reaches of the Highlands, much deeper than his illustrious grandfather had ever been able to do, and this time the English did not fall into the trap of trying to fight a guerrilla war with a conventional army. It was increasingly clear to Philip VI of France that not only had Edward of England no intention of abiding by the treaty of Northampton, but he had no intention of joining a crusade either.

By 1336, Edward had secured his northern borders against the Scots and had quietly built up a series of alliances with states bordering France, some owing allegiance not to Philip VI but to the Holy Roman Emperor (rather less holy after being excommunicated, but powerful nonetheless). The enthusiasm of these allies was directly proportional to the distance from France: the German states with the River Meuse between them and France were all for it; the Count of Flanders, next door to France, less so. Once more the threat of stopping exports of English wool was deployed to bring the Flemings into line. In France, litigation in the courts was chipping away at the rights of English cities and bishoprics in the disputed lands, and thanks to the Pope, Philip was the owner of a large fleet of ships. Since 1309 the papacy had been based in Avignon in southern France, whence it had moved to escape the infighting and machinations of the great Roman families who had hitherto dominated the office. From then until the return to Rome (in 1378), all the Popes would be French, and so would an increasing number of cardinals, often relatives of the reigning pope. Although the south of France was very different both in language and culture from the north, where king and government lay, the English tended to assume that popes were in the French king's pocket and while paying lip service to the papacy regarded any of its secular actions with suspicion. Pope John XXII was querulous and superstitious but a shrewd amasser of riches, and when he died in December 1334 his treasury was found to be full to overflowing. John's successor, Benedict XII, concealed behind an obese and drunken exterior a sharp political antenna, and in order to keep the peace in Europe and direct French and English warlike tendencies externally towards the recovery of the Holy Land, rather than internally towards each other, he had happily financed the building of a fleet to transport the proposed Anglo-French crusading army.

Then, in March 1336, the pope cancelled the crusade. He had concluded that he could not keep the peace between England and France, and that if Edward of England was not going to join an expedition, then the French king could not take his army abroad. That being so, Benedict might as well cancel the crusade, and rescind his authorisation for the clergy to be taxed to finance it. Philip now had a fleet to use for other purposes, and the ships began to move from Marseilles to the Channel ports. The English knew very well that the move could only presage a sea-born invasion of England, and Edward began to take measures to deal with it. Although English kings had long styled themselves 'Lords of the English Sea' by the time of Edward III it was an empty title, and at this period of English history there was no great maritime tradition to fall back on. From 1066 until King John lost his lands in France, England controlled directly or through alliances most of the Atlantic coast, and while after that navies were occasionally raised when invasion threatened, they were swiftly disbanded when the threat had passed. It was not that the English were unaware of the security of their sea routes – ships plying between Bordeaux and England hugged the coast rather than cross the Bay of Biscay, hence the importance of a friendly Brittany – it was just that they could not afford to spend much on it. Edward III owned but a handful of ships, with masters (often unpaid for long periods), but no crews, and in the event of a naval threat the defence of the nation at sea had depended upon the Cinque Ports. By ancient decree these (currently) five ports, in exchange for various customs and taxation privileges, were required to provide fifty-seven vessels between them for fifteen days. In fact, most of the ports had silted up, many of the ships they could provide ostensibly for war were in fact fishing vessels, and evasion of their obligations was widespread. In practice, the king would have to requisition ships from elsewhere – Great Yarmouth was now far more important as a port than any of the Cinque Ports and most of the ships would come from there.

Command of English navies was vested in two admirals, that of the North and that of the South. The posts were usually held either by soldiers, who knew a lot about fighting on land but little about war on the sea, or influential magnates, who might know very little about any sort of war. Most of the ships impressed for the English navy were cogs, thought to have originally developed from Viking longships. Cogs were wide-beamed, shallow-draught merchant vessels with one mast and a square-rigged sail, built of oak and with a stern rudder. Divided into various sizes ranging from 'up to 10 tons' to 'over 120 tons' most were relatively small, although there were cogs of 300 tons.[*] Being square-rigged, the cog could not sail into the wind, nor was it very manoeuvrable, but it could carry a considerable quantity of cargo, was reasonably resistant to bad weather and heavy seas, and could put in to estuaries and bays that a ship with a deeper draught could not. Most of those assembled to counter the threat of the French fleet were of 100 tons displacement, sixty feet long and twenty wide, with a crew of twenty-five sailors and a fighting element of archers or men at arms. Once taken into the king's service, stern castles and fore castles – wooden towers front and rear – and crows' nests were added which would be manned by archers and stone throwers, for English naval tactics were simple: ram any enemy ship, sink it or board it, attack the crew and chuck their bodies alive or dead overboard.

On 24 May 1337, King Philip announced the confiscation of Aquitaine, stated to be as punishment for Edward's failure to fulfil his obligations as a vassal of the French king. It is this act that can be taken as the beginning of the Hundred Years War. The English response was to despatch an advance party to the Low Countries

---

[*] By comparison, a modern Type 23 frigate of the Royal Navy displaces 4,800 tons.

to prepare for the reception of an English army which Edward intended to land there later in the year. Eighty-five ships crewed by 2,000 seamen carrying 1,500 soldiers and a large cargo of wool which would be sold to pay for the escapade set sail from Sandwich in November under Sir Walter Manny. Admiral of the North and responsible for all ports from the Thames to Berwick, Manny was an early example of the sort of men who would make their reputations and fortunes in the coming war. In his mid to late twenties in 1337, he was personally brave, unheeding of danger, reckless, flamboyant, and as greedy as everyone else at the time, but a competent commander and a good leader of men withal.

On 16 July 1338 Edward of England sailed with the main body of the army from Walton-on-the-Naze, south of Harwich on the Essex coast. Having landed at Antwerp the king processed to Coblenz, where in a lavish ceremony the Holy Roman Emperor Louis of Bavaria – whose anti-French and anti-Papal stance was reinforced by a hefty English bribe – appointed Edward as overlord of all the emperor's fiefs west of the Rhine. Even Edward's flat refusal to kiss the emperor's foot could not mar the occasion. It was now too late for campaigning that year and so having promised the rulers of the minor states supposedly now allied to him large subsidies for the provision of troops, Edward ordered them to concentrate their contingents north of Brussels in July the following year. The English court settled down in Antwerp for the winter, leaving the king's clerical staff to reply to the remonstrance of the pope who objected to Edward's dealings with the excommunicated Emperor. The pope pointed out that previous English kings had come to grief by trusting too much to foreign advice, a clear reference to Edward's father's fixation with Piers Gaveston.

It was not until September 1339 that Edward's army was ready to move, and even then, not all the promised participants had turned up. The campaign was exhausting and expensive, and it achieved nothing. The French could not be coaxed into battle and the end of the campaigning season found Edward angry, frustrated and increasingly in debt. His priority now was to raise enough money to continue the war, and also to persuade Flanders that neutrality was not an option. On 23 January 1340, in the marketplace in Ghent, Edward III proclaimed himself King of England and France. The French fleur-de-lys were now incorporated into the English royal coat of arms,[*] quartered with the English lions, and Edward took as his motto *Dieu et Mon Droit* – God and My Right – which has been and remains the motto of English and British sovereigns to this day. In England, Edward's claim was not universally approved. There was widespread distrust and indeed hatred of France, and Parliament had to enact a statute saying that in no circumstances, now or ever in the future, could any Englishman be subject to the laws of France.

---

[*] And stayed there until it was removed and replaced by the white horse of Hanover when England agreed to recognise the French republic in 1802, which meant giving up the claim to the French throne, held ever since that first claiming in 1340.

41

Chapter Three – First Blood

Although Philip had no intention of meeting the English army in open battle, in northern France fighting was going on in Gascony, French troops were besieging English castles in the Agenais, and they were active at sea too. Between 1337 and 1339 Rye, Folkestone, Dover, Harwich, Plymouth and the Isle of Wight were all subject to sudden French landings, followed by a brief period of pillage, rape and murder before the raiders set fire to what would burn and took to sea again. In 1338 they took most of the Channel Islands, and held them until 1340, and in 1338 they also captured England's largest ship, the king's own cog *Christopher*, along with the *Edward*. While the English responded by equally bloody raids on Le Treport and Boulogne, no town on England's east and south coasts was safe from French raids, usually by galleys which being powered by rowers were less subject to wind or tide than were English cogs. Added to that was Edward's financial situation, which was precarious. So far, the cost of procuring allies and sending an English expeditionary force to Europe and keeping it there had been met by loans, mainly from Italian bankers and English and Flemish merchants, but these sources were drying up, some loans were coming due for repayment, and more recent loans only went to repay old ones. Moreover, new ones could only be obtained at exorbitant rates of interest, and the wool brought over by Manny had not fetched as much as had been hoped. Things were so serious that Edward actually pawned the crown of England in Bruges: he had to tilt the balance of the war in his favour quickly, and the only solution was to raise more money from England and to bring over an army large enough to force a battle. In February 1340, a month after proclaiming himself King of France, Edward returned to England to raise funds. It was a humiliating departure: he had to agree to his queen and a number of his nobles remaining behind as surety for the loans, and he had to promise that he would return with the money, or, if without it, that he would subject himself to detention until it was found.

In the almost two years that Edward had been out of England, Parliament had increasingly begun to question the cost of the war, laying down all sorts of conditions before granting yet another tax. Edward met Parliament in March 1340 and deployed his extraordinary ability in managing public opinion to charm the legislators. Explaining that if the money was not raised then his honour would be destroyed, his lands in France lost and he himself imprisoned for debt, and assuring all that he had no intention of combining the two kingdoms nor of taking any action in England in his capacity as King of France, Edward asked for, and received, a tax of a ninth. This, in addition, to more loans squeezed from the London merchants and a levy on the clergy would be sufficient for him to carry on the war. He did not even discuss Parliament's conditions, agreeing to them all without argument.

The troops being assembled to reinforce those already in Europe were a mix of men raised by feudal array, volunteers and paid professionals, both men-at-arms and archers. The reported numbers of men in medieval armies are notoriously unreliable, and the number of English ships said by contemporary chronicles to have been mustered for the crossing vary from 147 to 260, but as the number of French ships is generally agreed to be around 200 and all chroniclers of both sides agree that the French fleet outnumbered that of the English, then 150 is probably the most the English could have had. If we allow that around fifty ships would have been carrying horses, stores and the ladies going out to join the queen, and that a 100 ton cog could carry at most 100 men of whom twenty-five would be crew, then the maximum number of soldiers might have been around 5,000 in the proportion of three archers to two men-at-arms.

By the time Edward and his fleet were ready to leave England, in June 1340, the English knew that the French fleet had been moved to Sluys, now silted up but then the main port for Bruges and northeast of it at the mouth of the Zwin on the south side of the Honde estuary. As the only purpose of stationing the fleet there would be for an invasion of England, or at the very least to prevent an English army from crossing the channel, Edward decided that he would meet the threat head-on and rather than avoiding the

French ships and landing at Dunkirk or Ostend he would do battle with them. This was an audacious plan indeed, and when Edward suggested it the Chancellor, Archbishop Stratford, argued strongly against it. When he could not change the king's mind, he resigned his office and returned the great seal of England to the king.[*] Edward summoned his most experienced Admiral, Robert Morley, and asked his opinion. Morley had served Edward II and had been party to the coup that deposed him, initially serving on land in Edward III's Scottish wars before taking to the sea. He had shown himself a most accomplished organiser and leader of raids on the French coast and was appointed Admiral of the North in February 1339. Morley pointed out the dangers of the king's plan and advised against it. His opinion was backed up by the very experienced Flemish seaman John Crabbe, who had originally been a mercenary pirate in the Scottish service and had been captured by the English and changed sides, and who was now the king's captain. Edward lost his temper and accused all three of plotting against him, telling them that they could stay at home, but he was going anyway, only being mollified when Morley and Crabbe announced that much as they opposed the caper, if the king went then so would they.

The story of the Battle of Sluys – the first major engagement of the Hundred Years War – is not one that springs to the lips of every English schoolboy; but in its way, it is as significant as the defeat of the Spanish armada in 1558. If it had been lost, then the 20,000 troops that Philip of France was amassing to invade England would have found nothing at sea to oppose them and precious little on land once they got there. Like Admiral Jellicoe at Jutland over half a millennium later, Edward III was the one man who could have lost the war in an afternoon.

Up to this point, despite the improving English ability to mount coastal raids, the French had been superior at sea, and had the Great Army of the Sea, as Philip termed it, been in the Channel a year earlier things might have been very different. Then, not only

---

[*] He was replaced by his brother, so the family were hardly disadvantaged.

would the French have mustered many more ships overall than they did now, but they would have had many more galleys, swift and manoeuvrable and far more suited to war at sea than the sluggish English cogs. Fortunately, a combination of a revolution in Genoa resulting in a regime no longer inclined to hire galleys and crews to the French, and English raids that had burned beached galleys at Boulogne, left the French with only six galleys, four of their own and two Genoese. In addition, the fleet had twenty-two oared barges, not as manoeuvrable as the galleys but more easily handled than the cogs nonetheless, seven sailing ships specifically built as naval vessels, and 167 requisitioned merchantmen. Manning the ships were around 19,000 soldiers and sailors, although only about 500 crossbowmen and 150 men at arms were professional soldiers, the rest being mariners, militia, and recently impressed recruits.

Knowing that Edward was intending to sail for the Low Countries, the best alternatives open to the French admirals were to blockade English ports or to catch the English fleet at sea and annihilate it. In the event, they did neither. The two French admirals, Quiéret and Béhuchet, elected to take up a defensive posture across the mouth of the three mile wide estuary running southwest from the island of Cadzand with their ships in three lines, chained together. Béhuchet, a short fat Norman, had started life as a civil servant before showing considerable ability as a leader of raids on the English coast. Quiéret was also an experienced sailor. Both men should have known better, for what they were doing was giving up the opportunity of fighting a sea battle, at which the French were far better than the English despite the shortage of galleys. Instead, they were giving the English an opportunity to fight a land battle on ships, and the English were very much better at fighting on land than the French. The two men did not get on personally, but the third commander in the Great Army of the Sea, a Genoese mercenary named Pietro Barbanero, Barbenoire, Barbevaire or Barbavera depending on the source, and the most experienced practitioner of naval warfare of them all, urged that such a defensive deployment gave no room for the ships to manoeuvre and that the fleet should put to sea and make use of its numerical advantage to fight the English well away from the shore. He was ignored.

The English fleet sailed from the mouth of the River Orwell at first light on 22 June 1340 with the king aboard the cog *Thomas*, and hove-to off the Flemish coast the following morning at, according to Edward's despatches, the hour of 'tierce' or 0900 hrs. The two fleets could see each other, and King Edward first ordered the church militant, in the form of the Bishop of Lincoln, to go ashore, ride the ten miles or so to Bruges and encourage the Flemings to attack the French from the shore once the English fleet attacked from the sea. Three knights were also landed to observe the French fleet and count the number and disposition of the ships. By early the next morning, 24 June, Edward knew the strength and layout of the French fleet. He had also received the Bishop of Lincoln's unwelcome news that the citizens of Bruges were adamant that on no account should the English attack such a huge French fleet, for to do so would court disaster. Rather, they said, Edward should wait for a few days until he could be reinforced by Flemish ships. The king ignored that advice but as to attack at once would mean sailing into the sun, Edward decided to tack out to sea and position himself where the wind and the tide would be at his back. This, and the redisposition of the fleet into attack formation, took most of the day. Some sources say that the manoeuvring was interpreted by the French as an English retreat and that they began to unchain their own ships in order to pursue, and Barbanero certainly advised a move out to sea. In any event, many French ships were still chained together, and their fleet was still in a defensive posture when the English, with the wind, the tide and the sun behind them, struck.

Edward had arranged his fleet in three lines, each line with the ships in line abreast, with one ship full of men at arms – infantry – flanked by two of archers. The archers were on the fore and stern castles and in the crow's nests and as the fleets closed a storm of arrows began to cause casualties amongst the French. Their crossbowmen replied, but there were insufficient numbers of them and with their much slower rate of fire, they were ineffective. When the lines of ships crashed into each other the English sailors swung their grappling irons and the infantry began to board. This was difficult, as many of the French ships were higher than those of the English, particularly the Spanish vessels of Philip's Castilian ally, but once on board the raw sailors were no match for the English men at arms, most of them with fighting skills honed by the Scottish wars. With sword, mace, short spear and bill, the English infantry captured ship after ship in the first line, including retaking the cog *Christopher*. Once the colours of Philip of Valois were struck and replaced by the lions and fleur-de-lys of England, panic set in amongst the second line of smaller ships and less experienced crews. By nightfall, most of the ships of the second French line had been captured and those of the third were trying to make their escape. Many soldiers and sailors jumped overboard to escape the ferocity of the English attack but many of those who managed to swim ashore were bludgeoned to death by the waiting Flemings, while those who could not swim (most) were drowned, as were many who could swim but were weighed down by armour. In the darkness, some French ships got away, including Barbanero's galleys, but the next morning any remaining in the estuary were swiftly accounted for, and altogether 190 French ships were captured or sunk.

It was a great and overwhelming victory. Edward, and most contemporary chronicles, attributed it to the grace of God, but in truth the French were beaten by themselves, throwing away their advantages in numbers and seamanship by confining themselves to the estuary. Once they had thus limited themselves, the superiority of English archers' firepower and the experience and fighting abilities of the English infantry once they had boarded the French ships were decisive. Sources vary as to the extent of the butcher's bill. Most of the chronicles give figures between 20,000 and 30,000 French dead which are almost certainly far too high. But while a beaten army on land can run away, the only escape at sea is into it, so there may have been as many as 10,000 French dead, wounded and prisoners, or about half the total number engaged, and for days afterwards bodies were being washed ashore. Quiéret was killed in the fighting but Béhuchet was recognised and held by his captor in the hope of ransom. It was not to be: the scourge of the English coastal towns was not going to get away so lightly and Edward had him hanged on the mast of his own ship. English casualties were remarkably light considering the intensity of the ship-to-ship fighting; there were between 400 and 600 killed and wounded, including the king himself who sustained minor wounds to his thigh and hand. While the French could and would still raid English coastal towns, the threat of a full-scale invasion had gone.

To the English, all the auguries for a successful campaign in northern France now looked good. Edward decided to capture the frontier city of Tournai himself, while Robert of Artois,* with Flemish troops bolstered by a small contingent of English archers would take the city of St Omer. All came to naught. Robert was unable to take St Omer and had to retire back to join Edward, and Edward was unable to take Tournai as he had no siege train. He also had his usual problems over money and had once more to appeal to parliament in England for another subsidy. There, public opinion, while supportive of the war, was fiercely opposed to yet more taxation: '*Wherefore you shall know the very truth: the inner love of the people was turned into hate and the common prayers into cursing, for cause that the common people were strongly aggrieved*' as one chronicle put it. A grant was forthcoming, but not enough to keep the armies in the field nor to conduct a lengthy siege. In mid-September, with the weather deteriorating, supplies running low and the less committed allies beginning to hedge their bets, the pope proposed a truce to last until the summer of 1341. Edward was glad to accept and slink back to England. It was an inglorious end to what had been such a promising start, and it would not be for another six years that Edward III would achieve such a devastating victory as that of Sluys, and then it would be on land – the Battle of Crécy.

The story of the Hundred Years War is in many ways that of the professional versus the amateur, with increasing professionalisation of English armies followed, usually all too late,

* A French noble, he had fallen out with Philip and sought refuge in England.

by those of France. The Battle of Crécy saw the beginnings of a genuine revolution in military affairs, for by the time of Edward I the English military system, a fusion of the pre-conquest Anglo-Saxon military organisation with Norman feudalism, was beginning to creak. The Anglo-Saxons had depended on semi-professional household troops employed directly by the king, supported by the *Fyrd* or militia. This was a part-time force embodied when danger threatened and which could be required either to operate solely within its own shire, or, like those elements which accompanied King Harold to Stamford Bridge and down again to Hastings in 1066, nationwide. The Norman feudal system, on the other hand, presupposed that all land belonged to the king and was granted to his supporters, who in turn owed him military service. This service was expressed in terms of the number of knights the landholder, or tenant-in-chief, was required to provide for a fixed time, usually forty days. Often, the tenant-in-chief would sub-allocate land to his tenants who then took on the military service obligation. Each knight was required to provide his own equipment – armour (initially mail, giving way progressively to plate), helmet, sword, shield and lance, and at least one horse. Each knight brought his retinue with him: a page to look after and clean his armour, a groom to care for his horses, and probably a manservant to look after him. Often there would be numerous armed followers, frequently described as esquires, or well-bred young men aspiring to knighthood. Bishops and monasteries also had a military obligation, usually, but not always, commuted for a cash payment in lieu. The number of knights required from each land holding reduced steadily during the post-conquest period, presumably because knights and their equipment became more expensive, and by 1217 a total of 115 tenants-in-chief are recorded as producing between them 470 knights.

When Edward III came to the throne the English peerage had not developed into the modern system of Baron, Viscount, Earl, Marquis and Duke, and it was Edward who created the first English duke – his eldest son, the Prince of Wales. After the Conquest, the Normans took over the existing Anglo-Saxon title of earl (from the Scandinavian Jarl) although it was given to

Normans and not to those who held the rank before the conquest, and they also introduced the rank of baron, who came below an earl. The term 'knight' did not have the exactitude that it does today, when we have two types of knight: the knight bachelor dubbed by the monarch and entitled to be described as 'Sir Thomas Voletrouser' and his wife as 'Lady Voletrouser' and who holds the title for his lifetime only; and the hereditary knight baronet, also entitled to be described as Sir Thomas but with the abbreviation Bart. or Bt. after the name. The latter honour is relatively recent, having been introduced by King James I as a money-raising scheme in 1611. During the medieval period, the honours system was much more elastic. A military knight had not necessarily been dubbed but was able to afford the cost of knight's equipment and was probably a landholder. Assuming that he did reasonably well he would almost certainly be dubbed eventually, often on the eve of battle. A knighthood banneret, a title that lapsed in the seventeenth century, could only be awarded on the field of battle and only if the king was present, and it entitled the holder to display a rectangular banneret, as opposed to the triangular pennon of lower ranking knights, and his own coat of arms or heraldic device. The men who filled the knightly class were brought up to and trained for battle, but it was battle as individuals – tourneys and jousts for real – and under the feudal system there was a real difficulty in getting them to act as a team, or to persuade them to adopt a common tactical doctrine.

The knights – whether dubbed or not – were what we would call the officers of the army, while the Other Ranks were provided by commissions of array, or conscription, from able-bodied men of the hundreds or shires. Again, these were only required to serve for a limited period, and there were frequent arguments as to whether they could be compelled to serve outside their own locality, and whether it was a local or national (i.e. royal) responsibility to feed and pay them.

When the king knew personally all or most of the landholders in the kingdom the feudal system worked reasonably well. It sufficed for dynastic squabbles and raids from Scotland, but as time went on it could not cope with expeditions abroad, or with sieges that lasted more than forty days, nor could it provide permanent garrisons. Men could not reasonably be expected to be absent from their homes during the planting season, nor for the harvest, and this greatly restricted the scope and duration of any military campaign. Even as early as the reign of Henry II, in 1171, the king faced his rebellious sons with forces that, while largely composed of men carrying out their feudal dues, included 'knights serving for wages' and as time went on the transition from a feudal host where the officers served as part of their obligation to their overlord, to an army where all served for pay was an inevitable progression given that kings of England fought their wars abroad. Once soldiers (of any rank) serve for pay, rather than almost as a favour, they can be ordered to arm themselves and fight in a certain way, they can be sent to where the king wants them rather than where they want to go, and, as long as the money holds out, loyalty is assured. It was Edward I who began this professionalisation of the army. Eventually, he paid everybody except those whom we would term generals, and it was his efforts that laid the groundwork for the great victories of his grandson Edward III against French armies which were usually far larger, but still raised under a semi-feudal system.

One way of raising soldiers once the feudal system had irreparably broken down was to hire foreign mercenaries, and there were lots of those ready to sell their services to the highest bidder. Most of the mercenary bands were from areas where nothing much grew, like Brittany, or where there was overcrowding such as in Flanders or Brabant, or where other career paths were limited, as in Genoa. The difficulty was an inherent English dislike of foreigners, so while there were contingents from Brittany and Flanders in English armies abroad, there were very few actually employed in England. Even the Welsh, who provided large numbers of soldiers for Edward's wars, tended to be mustered and then marched off to the embarkation ports as speedily as possible.

It was not only the move from feudal to paid service that marked a revolution in military affairs, at least in England, but the composition of armies too. During the feudal period, the major arm was the heavy cavalry, composed of armoured knights on armoured horses who provided shock action and could generally ride through and scatter any footmen in their way. As socially the cavalry were regarded as several cuts above the infantry, who were often poorly equipped and scantily trained militia, this held true for a very long time. The cavalryman wore mail or latterly plate armour, carried a sword, lance and shield, and was mounted on either a destrier or a courser. The destrier, or great horse, was not, as is sometimes alleged, the Shire horse or the Percheron of today. Rather it was similar to today's Irish Draught. Short coupled, rather cobby, with strong quarters and well up to weight, the destrier was probably between 14 and 15 hands,[*] although some of the horse armour at the Royal Armouries at Leeds is made for a horse of 15 to 16 hands.[†] The courser was similar, but lighter and cheaper. Destriers are sometimes said to have been entires, and the Bayeux tapestry certainly shows them as uncastrated, but this seems unlikely. An uncastrated horse is far less tractable than a gelding or a mare and the depiction of the complete animal in paintings and tapestries of the period may simply be symbolic – our horses are male and rampant and so are we.

There has been much discussion as to the role of the stirrup in equestrian warfare. Some authorities state that it was only with the invention of the stirrup that the cavalryman could be anything other than an appendage to an army: useful for reconnaissance and communications but incapable of serious fighting because only when able to brace against the stirrups could a man deliver a weighty blow without falling off. It is probable that those who make this assertion have little experience of riding. While the stirrup is a useful aid to balance when the horse does something unintended and unexpected, it is by no means essential and it

---

[*] Horses are measured without shoes from the top of the withers vertically to the ground, the unit of measurement being the hand of four inches, thus a horse described as being 14h 2 means one of fourteen hands and two inches.

[†] But this may be intended for a parade horse, rather than one to be ridden in battle.

would have been very difficult to fall out of a stirrup-less Roman saddle, with its high pommel and cantle. Similarly, the armchair nature of the medieval saddle, even with stirrups, made for a very safe seat except if the horse fell, when the rider, rather than being thrown clear as he would hope to be in a modern saddle, would be trapped under the horse risking a broken pelvis or his throat cut by an opportunistic infantryman. All the depictions of the armoured medieval cavalryman show him riding with a straight leg and very long leathers, so he could not brace against the stirrups in any case. It seems, to this author at least, that the usefulness of the stirrup was in mounting the horse when there was no mounting block available or when the weight of armour made it impossible to vault astride the withers. In addition to his warhorse, the armoured warrior would also have a palfrey, a hack to be ridden when not in battle and not encumbered by armour, and a pack horse to carry his kit. Fodder for a minimum of three horses per man and rations for him and the host of camp followers, to say nothing of the cost of horses and armour, made the armoured knight a very expensive fellow. However, it was not cost that forced his decline and eventual banishment from the battlefield altogether but advances in technology and the quality of the infantry.

During the Welsh wars, the English began to have doubts as to the merits of a largely cavalry army: the hills and valleys of Wales did not lend themselves to flat-out charges or to wide envelopment, and Welsh infantry spearmen were generally able to put up a stout defence unless surprised and scattered. There were other indications: at Courtrai in 1302 a Flemish infantry army had roundly defeated the flower of the French heavy cavalry by digging ditches across the approaches to their position and then standing on the defensive. The French duly charged, the impetus was destroyed by horses falling into or breaking legs in the ditches, and the Flemish won the day. As far as the English were concerned it was Bannockburn that began to bring it home that well organised and equipped infantry, however ill-bred, could see off a mounted host if they could bring their enemy to battle on the ground of their choosing. There, on 23 June 1314, Robert Bruce's Scottish army took up a dismounted position at one end of a flat field, with both his flanks protected by woods and marshes. His men dug holes and ditches, three feet deep by three feet wide, across the inviting approaches, camouflaged them with wooden trellises covered with grass and leaves, and waited. Having had his vanguard repulsed on that day while trying to move around the Scottish flank to get to and relieve the siege of Stirling, Edward II ordered, as expected, a cavalry charge on 24 June. It was a disaster. The Scots infantry did not flee, and by presenting a wall of pikes, prevented even those horsemen who did negotiate the obstacles from getting anywhere near them. Eight years later Sir Andrew Harclay's wedge of pikemen supported by archers stopped Thomas of Lancaster's infantry and cavalry from getting across the only bridge over the River Ure at Boroughbridge, while an attempt to put cavalry across by a nearby ford was stopped by archers alone.

That the English had absorbed the lessons of Bannockburn and Boroughbridge was confirmed at Dupplin Moor and Halidon Hill. At Dupplin Moor, six miles south-west of Perth, on 11 August 1332, the 1,500 strong army of the Disinherited nominally commanded by Edward Balliol but with English advisers there with the unofficial blessing of Edward III, defeated the Bruce army of 3,000 commanded by Donald, Earl of Mar. The Disinherited lost two English knights and thirty-three men-at-arms. The Scots losses are unknown but included three earls and must have been many hundreds. On 19 July the following year at Halidon Hill, two miles northwest of Berwick on Tweed, an English army of around 4,000 led by Edward III in person roundly defeated Sir Archibald Douglas's 5,000 strong Scots army. Again, English losses were negligible – one knight, one esquire and ten infantrymen of various sorts, while Douglas and five Scots earls were killed and an unknown number of lesser nobles and soldiers, perhaps as many as 1,000 all told. After Halidon Hill there was no one left in Scotland capable of raising an army and Robert Bruce's kingdom was effectively at an end.

Both Dupplin Moor and Halidon Hill had a number of factors in common, which enabled English armies to inflict crushing defeats on greater numbers, and those factors were to be incorporated into English military doctrine for the Hundred Years War. In each case, archers formed the largest portion of the armies, and the victorious commanders chose to stand on a piece of ground where their own flanks were secure, and which restricted the frontage of the enemy. At Dupplin Moor this was effected by taking up a defensive position at the head of a steep-sided valley; at Halidon Hill Edward's right flank was covered by the sea while on his left was marshy ground with a river flowing through it. In both cases, English forces fought on foot, including King Edward himself at Halidon Hill, in two ranks with archers on the flanks and in both cases the archers concentrated their arrow storms on the advancing Scots flanks, forcing them to close in towards their centre and reducing their frontage and hence their shock effect still more. When the Scots finally reached the English infantry line (or failed to do so at Halidon Hill) they had suffered so many casualties from the archers that their cohesion was broken, and they were repulsed and fled. The pursuit was taken up by the English remounting their horses and following the defeated Scots. The policy of dismounting and standing on the defensive on carefully chosen ground, using archers to prevent outflanking moves and break up enemy attacking formations, and presenting a solid mass of infantry in a two or four-deep line to meet the attacking remnants was the recipe for the great English victories of the war. In fact, it was only when the English overreached themselves, and the French finally began to learn from their own defeats, that English military supremacy began to wane.

Technology came in the shape of the longbow. Bows and arrows are as old as prehistoric man: the simplest of missile weapons, they are depicted in Palaeolithic and Neolithic cave paintings and archaeological excavations have uncovered bows and arrows dating back to the third millennium BC. Bows were in use by Roman auxiliaries and light hunting bows were in use by both sides at Hastings in 1066. Quite how and where the short bow, drawn back to the chest and with its limited range and penetrating power, mutated into the English longbow is uncertain: it would not have been a sudden change, and it may have first been used by the southern Welsh, and probably by hunters rather than soldiers. It was gradually, and eventually enthusiastically, adopted by the

English, and as a reluctance to spend money on defence is not confined to twenty-first century British governments, its cheapness would have appealed. The longbow would become the English weapon of mass destruction; it was consistently ignored by England's enemies, who would consistently be slaughtered by it. There had long been statutes that required all free men to keep weapons at home and to practise archery regularly at the village butts, for the longbow was not something that could be picked up and used by anybody. Archers began to develop their skills as children, gradually increasing the size and 'pull' of their bows as they grew up. Exhumed bodies of medieval archers show greatly developed, or overdeveloped, shoulder and back muscles.

The standard longbow was made of yew wood, either native English yew or imported from Ireland, Spain or Italy and approximated in length to the height of the archer. Thus, there would not have been very many that were six feet in length, as modern reproductions are, rather the average would have been around five feet two or three. While originally the same craftsman would manufacture bows and arrows this soon diverged into two trades, the bowyers who made bows and the fletchers who made arrows, each with their own guild. The bow had a pull of around 100 lbs and shot a 'cloth yard' arrow out to an effective range of about 300 yards. There is dispute as to exactly how long a cloth yard was, the measurement being one used by Flemish weavers, many of whom came to England encouraged by Edward III, and definitions vary from 27 ¼ inches to 37 inches, the latter supposedly codified by Edward VI, the short-lived son of Henry VIII, while some sources describe an arrow as being an ell in length. As an English ell was 45 inches this seems unlikely. Whatever the length of the arrow, and the shorter seems more realistic, its construction was a skilled affair, requiring the fletcher to obtain good straight wood for the shaft, usually ash, cut it to the correct length, affix the arrowhead and the feathers to stabilise the arrow in flight. Three pinion feathers per arrow were required, which came from a goose. As a goose only had six pinion feathers, three on each wing, and as they only regrew on moulting annually, and as hundreds of thousands of arrows were ordered during the wars, the goose population in the kingdom must have been considerable.

Arrow heads came in two basic types: one to pierce flesh with broad barbs, and the other, much narrower with a sharp point and no barbs, to penetrate armour. While the arrow was said to be capable of going through an inch of oak at a hundred yards it would not have gone through plate armour except at relatively close range and at a flat trajectory. The usual way of employing archers was to mass them and have them shoot volleys at a forty-five degree angle, thus obtaining maximum range and ensuring that they struck from above. While this might not immediately kill armoured cavalrymen, it would wound them, panic their horses, and generally discourage an enemy from pressing home his charge. As a competent archer was expected to be able to discharge ten arrows a minute, the 7,000 or so archers that King Edward would take on the Crécy expedition in 1346 could produce a horrifying arrow storm of 35,000 arrows every thirty seconds!

The other missile weapon in general use was the crossbow. This was made of a composite of wood and horn, and sometimes steel, and shot a bolt, or quarrel, of iron, steel or ash with more force to a greater range and with more accuracy than the longbow. As its rate of discharge was only around two quarrels a minute, due to the effort and the length of time needed to pull the bowstring back to engage with the trigger, the English generally only employed it as a defensive weapon in castles and fortified places. It could, however, be shot from behind cover, unlike the longbow, and unlike the longbow required little training to use. In the field, crossbowmen carried a large shield, a *pavisse*. This was as high as a man and had an easel-type leg at the back which allowed it to stand up unsupported by the soldier, and which afforded him cover while he reloaded. The French did have some longbowmen but presumably considered the training and development to be not worth the effort and, still fighting their wars with a feudal host, employed large numbers of mercenary crossbowmen, to their detriment as we shall see.

In England, contracts for very large numbers of bows and arrows were let and in 1341 when the king had returned from

France and was gearing up for another foray there, 7,700 bows and 12,800 sheaves of arrows were purchased and stored in the Tower of London. A sheaf was twenty-four arrows, so this was an astonishing total of 397,000 arrows, with the feathers of 51,200 geese; but it was still only four minutes of shooting for the 10,000 archers that Edward was intending to take to France.

The other major element of the English military machine was the man-at-arms, the successor of the heavily armoured mounted knight. Men-at-arms were mainly of gentle birth – ranging from actual knights, or those hoping to become knights, to esquires or minor gentry, usually in the proportion of one knight to four others. Like the mounted archers they moved on horseback but fought on foot. Once the transition from mounted to dismounted battle took place the shield grew smaller and eventually was dispensed with altogether. Men-at-arms were still well protected, although unlike their French equivalents mainly in mail, rather than plate, armour. While equipped with swords, the main weapon was the halberd, or half pike, although a variety of axes, maces and daggers were also carried. The men-at-arms were drawn up in two or four ranks, depending on the frontage to be covered, close together but not so close that they could not swing their weapons, and taking up thirty inches or so apiece.

While the heavy cavalry component had almost disappeared in English armies there was still a requirement for light cavalry, and these were the *hobilar*s, shown in the muster rolls as *armatti*, who were lightly armed and mounted on ponies or modern light hunter types. Their role was not to charge the enemy but to reconnoitre, patrol, find routes, forage for rations, collect intelligence and provide communications. With so much of the army now mounted there was of course a requirement for grooms and farriers to accompany the army, to say nothing of the huge amount of forage that would either have to be shipped with the army or bought or sequestered on the ground. Other specialists would be miners for siege work, armourers to repair weapons and suits of armour, masons and carpenters to construct defences and build bridges, bowyers and fletchers to repair and replace the archers' necessities and even a military band. Edward III may also have had some early cannon, or gunpowder artillery, although the details are vague.

Chapter Four – To War

The army that Edward was gathering was made up of three types of soldier: those belonging to retinues, either the kings or those of magnates; paid contingents raised by individual contractors; and men summoned by commissions of array. There were two sorts of retinues: those composed of household troops and those indentured. Household retinues consisted of those men who were tenants of the lord and to whom they and their families owed a feudal obligation. These personal retinues would become less important as the war went on, but in the 1340s were still significant. Indentured retinues – sometimes unkindly referred to as 'bastard feudalism' – were those raised by an individual, who had to be of the rank of knight banneret or above, and its members were employed on contract, occasionally for a specific period, but more often to serve the lord in peace and war for life. The contract was written, laid down the wages and expenses to be paid and stipulated exactly what type of service was to be provided, including whether it was to be within England only or abroad, and usually included the proviso that a certain proportion of any ransom or plunder acquired was to go to the lord. Service was owed to that particular lord and could not be transferred to anyone else without the agreement of both parties. The contract was sealed and both parties kept a copy. Members of indentured retinues were required to be of the rank of knight or esquire and were required to wear the lord's badge or uniform. The retinues varied in size. The Earl of Northampton in 1341 undertook to provide 7 bannerets, 74 knights, 199 men-at-arms, 200 armed men (spearmen and *hobilar*s) and 100 archers, while the Earl of Derby in 1342 agreed to muster 5 bannerets, 50 knights, 144 esquires and 200 mounted archers, both forces a mix of household and indentured retinues. A less well-off member of the gentry like John Beauchamp produced a single knight (himself), 5 esquires, 6 men-at-arms and 4 mounted archers. As knights still had a feudal obligation it was in the government's interest to have lots of them, and there were various regulations to persuade those of means (lands worth £40 a year) to accept knighthood. To those who were going to war, whether as part of an overlord's retinue or of their own volition, knighthood was an advantage, for not only did it double the man's pay but a captured knight was more likely to be held for ransom rather than slaughtered out of hand. That said, the expense of armour, horses, servants and the other trappings of gentility did deter some, and fines were levied against those who turned knighthood down. When the king was strong and admired as Edward III was there were few who resisted becoming knights and contributing to the war effort, while the contrary had applied to his father Edward II.

Contract forces raised by the king and the government were similar to indentured retinues but without personal loyalty to an individual lord and were the first true professional or career soldiers. They might be considered the national army, as opposed to local or private armed bodies. An individual, usually referred to as a captain, contracted to produce a certain number of soldiers of a laid down type for a laid down period to serve in a particular area, and terms and conditions of service were laid down and agreed. Like indentured retinues, numbers varied widely: from Edward Montagu, captain, who in 1341 agreed to provide six knights, twenty men-at-arms, twelve spearmen and twelve archers for forty days for a total of £76, to men like Sir Hugh Calveley who could recruit a thousand soldiers.

In these early stages of the war soldiers raised by commissions of array – a system of conscription that had changed little since Saxon times – outnumbered those in retinues or under contract, although as time went on the army would become more and more composed of professionals. With the exception of those living in the coastal areas, all males aged between sixteen and sixty were liable to conscription organised by arrayers, who might be sergeants at arms (royal servants and more like mobile inspectors and troubleshooters rather than the senior non-commissioned officers they are today), knights of the king's household or local officials. Using the local authorities to select men was administratively simple but invited corruption, as local arrayers sought or were offered bribes to exempt those who did not wish to go, and often the men selected were quite unfit for military service. Sergeants at arms or the king's own officials were less susceptible to corruption and got a better quality of man, since having military experience themselves they knew the sort of man they wanted. Even then there were problems. Often the best men had already been recruited either into a local lord's retinue or into an indentured company. Additionally, despite various statutes, not everybody possessed weapons, which had to be provided or paid for locally, and it was a stipulation that those who did not serve were required to contribute towards the cost of those who did. Because of the difficulty of finding sufficient men by array there had to be incentives. These ranged from assuring pressed men that they could keep a certain proportion of the value of goods captured, usually up to £100, which was twenty years salary for a foot archer, and pardons for outlaws. If a man who was ordered to appear before the courts on a criminal charge consistently failed to appear, then he was declared outlaw, or 'without the law', which meant that, technically at least, depending on the seriousness of his alleged offence, he could be killed with impunity. Outlawry only applied to the man's county, so someone on the run had only to escape to the next county to be safe from retribution, but as an outlaw's goods and chattels were forfeit to the crown, it was not a comfortable state. The king, and only the king, could grant pardons in exchange for military service, although sensibly the pardon was usually withheld until the service was complete and the man's good behaviour attested to by his commander. In the year 1339 – 1340 a total of 850 charters of pardon were granted for military services rendered, of which around three quarters are estimated to be to murderers. Altogether perhaps up to ten percent of this early English army was made up of criminals working their passage to forgiveness.

Men raised by commissions of array were organised into *vintenaries*, or twenties, under a *vintenar* or junior officer, usually a knight but if not someone of military experience. Five *vintenaries* made a *centenary* commanded by a *centenar* who was mounted even if his troops were not. The nearest modern equivalent is the platoon and the company. We have little knowledge of how these men were trained, but clearly there must have been a training syllabus over and above weekly archery practice. While soldiers of the time did not march in step, they would have been required to move with a measured pace at a set rate of paces per minute, so that they could change formation without losing cohesion. The men would have had to have been made accustomed to moving and fighting as part of a team, to obey orders without question, to understand military terminology and to handle their weapons as the army demanded. Development of physical fitness and training in living in the field would not have been as important as they are for young British recruits today, but some understanding of field hygiene and first aid would presumably have been instilled.

Soldiers wearing a uniform are recognisable and hence easier to control and discipline, while finding it more difficult to desert, and while at this stage there was not a national uniform in the modern sense, many contingents were equipped to a common standard of dress. Welsh contingents were clothed in hats and quilted tunics that were white on one side and green on the other, the men of London wore red and white stripes, and many of the richer magnates, and even localities, vied with each other in the provision of uniform clothing. Mostly the men seem to have been clothed in various shades of white. But even if bodies for the same area were all uniformed to a greater or lesser extent, with the number of contingents in the army and the wearing of individual coats of arms on bannerets' surcoats, to say nothing of the standards and banners displayed by barons, earls and formation commanders, recognition in the heat of battle cannot have been easy. Edward III eventually reverted to his grandfather's practice of ordering all to wear an armband of the red cross of St George.

By now it was recognised that, lingering feudal obligations notwithstanding, officers and men of an army had to be paid. Rates of pay did vary somewhat depending upon the success or otherwise of recruitment and were expressed as daily rates (as British army rates of pay still are). A duke (and at first there was only one – the Prince of Wales) got 13 shillings and four pence, 13/4 (£0.67), an earl 8/- (£0.40), a knight banneret 4/- (£0.20), and a knight bachelor 2/- (£0.10). A man-at-arms who was not a knight received 1/- (£0.05), an English *vintenar*, a *hobilar* and a mounted archer 6d (£0.025) and a Welsh *vintenar*, a dismounted archer and an English light infantryman 3d (£0.0125). A Welsh spearman got 2d (£0.0083). Taking the numbers that they might command, then the duke might be a brigade commander, the earl a battalion commander, the banneret a company commander and the knight a platoon commander.

While of less importance after the Battle of Sluys, it was still necessary to guard against sea-borne raids. This was the responsibility of the Keepers of the Maritime Lands; officials in the counties bordering on the sea who were appointed by the king and who organised and commanded the Garde de la Mer, which combined dedicated coastal observers with a warning system and a callout in the event of a French landing. The warning system, put into operation if a landing was thought to be imminent, consisted of a line of beacons along the shore and stretching inland which were to be ignited if a landing was about to take place. Each beacon was attended by between four and six men, who manned an observation post consisting of two or three wine barrels filled with sand and stacked on top of each other with a watcher perched on top looking out to sea. Pitch was preferred to twigs in the beacons as less likely to be affected by rain, and churches were ordered that under normal circumstances only one bell was to be rung, the ringing of all the bells being the signal that a landing was happening. Men living in the Maritime Lands – defined as the coastal strip extending three leagues (nine miles) inland – were exempt from military service outside that area and owners of estates within the area were reminded that they must live on them, as they provided the officers in the event of a call out of the militia to counter an invasion. There were also arrangements whereby the militia of inland counties could be deployed to coastal counties if invasion threatened. One of the difficulties was the need to prevent residents of the Maritime Lands from leaving them, as many who lived on the Isle of Wight, and in Portsmouth and Southampton, areas regularly raided by the French, not unnaturally tried to do. These arrangements had changed little from pre-Norman times and while the system could cope with minor raids it is doubtful whether it could have done very much to counter a full scale invasion – fortunately, after Sluys it did not have to.

While Edward was raising money and an army to return to France, warfare had not stood still, for English troops were very much involved in Brittany, where the English supported one claimant to the dukedom, and the French another. It was important to ensure a client, or at least friendly Brittany, not only to preserve the security of the sea route from Aquitaine, but also to give Edward another point from where he could attack France when hostilities were resumed.

In England, preparations proceeded apace. While the army would attempt to live off the land in enemy territory and by local purchase in the country of an ally, the men would have to be fed while they waited to embark, while they were at sea and on landing until other arrangements could be made. Royal commissaries would purchase the necessary rations in bulk and have them delivered to the muster stations or ports of embarkation, or this might be delegated to the admiral in command of a fleet. Meat would usually be salted beef, pork, bacon and mutton, although beef on the hoof could also be bought and transported, while vegetables would be peas, beans and oats. Wheat would be bought but ground into flour before delivery. Cheese was bought by the 'wey', a wey being 26 stones, and large quantities of dried fish, mainly herring, were also supplied. The potato was, of course, unknown and its equivalent was bread, which was the staple for medieval man, who did not (unless he was very rich) eat from a plate but from a 'trencher' a flat, boat-shaped piece of bread. As wheat, which produced white flour, would only grow in ground that was well manured, white bread was restricted to the rich (the officers) while the lower ranks made do with black bread made from rye, or loaves made from barley or even from ground peas. Water was generally contaminated, unclean and the bearer of all sorts of illnesses, and so was only drunk in extremis. Instead, people drank ale, which was brewed from barley.[*] The barley was soaked until it germinated and produced malt, which was dried and ground and then mixed with hot water and allowed to ferment. The result was only very mildly alcoholic – certainly not of strength to have any effect – and the ration for a soldier or a sailor was one gallon per man per day. Many households brewed their own ale, although brewing was one of the few commercial activities open to women. There were, however, very few brewers who could supply the quantities needed by an army or a fleet. In 1340, when Yarmouth contracted to supply 30 ships for forty days to ply between England and Flanders, the 60,400 gallons for the 1,510 men of the ships' crews came from just three suppliers at a cost to the treasury of 1d a gallon.[†]

From late 1345 and into the spring of 1346, soldiers were ordered to muster points and then to the ports of embarkation, while the king's sergeants at arms were ordered to 'arrest' shipping and have it prepared to transport the army to France. The requisition of ships in this way was not popular with owners or merchants, as it interfered with trade and nor could it be done quickly. The ship would have to unload its cargo, often in an unintended port, be moved to Portsmouth, Winchelsea or Sandwich, prepared for the transport of troops and horses and then loaded with rations and equipment to await the arrival of the troops. Ships that were to become horse transports had to have extra wide gangways installed and stalls built on board for the horses. In Hampshire alone, orders were placed for twenty gangways and 1,000 hurdles to make the partitions for the stalls, plus nails, rings to tie the horses to and rope for halters.

---

[*] Beer, which is made from hops, was drunk in Europe at this time but not in England. In modern usage, the terms beer and ale are interchangeable except to the purist.

[†] Today a gallon of real ale (admittedly much stronger than its medieval ancestor) costs £22, an inflation factor of 5,280. A gallon in the 1340s cost a third of a day's pay for a foot archer and today it costs about a third of a day's pay for a mid-band private soldier, so perhaps the ale standard is the most accurate comparator of monetary values yet!

Soldiers conscripted by commissions of array were to be from the counties 'citra Trent', south of the river Trent, only, as the Scottish threat could not be discounted. The men were ordered to muster points in their own localities and then, when enough had reported to justify detaching an officer or *vintenar* to command them, sent off to one of the embarkation ports. On 2 January 1346, thirty men from Salisbury were despatched to Sandwich and took six days to cover the 130 miles; men from Stafford took seven days to cover the 140 miles to the same port; and men from Shaftsbury took twelve days to get to Winchelsea via Southampton, a distance of 155 miles. Men were therefore expected to march up to twenty miles a day along rough roads and tracks while carrying their weapons and personal kit. Physical fitness was not a problem. On arrival and waiting at the muster point, and while on the march to the port, the wages of the arrayed soldiers were the responsibility of their counties, but once they arrived at the port then they went onto 'king's wages'. As in some cases they had to wait for long periods until other contingents arrived or until the weather was suitable, their presence was no doubt welcomed by prostitutes and tavern keepers, although perhaps not so enthusiastically by others.

The total numbers assembled by Edward for his 1346 invasion of France are not easy to come by: many original records, pay rolls and the like have been lost and chroniclers seem to have plucked a number out of the air, nearly always wildly exaggerated. The best guess is that Edward's army totalled around 16,500 combatants, perhaps slightly more, plus specialists (standard bearers, trumpeters, chaplains, physicians, farriers, miners, gunners, artisans various and the Bishop of Durham, whose pay rate was 6/8 or £0.33 a day). Of this, 7,700 odd were men of retinues, either feudal or indentured or contracted companies, while around 8,600 were men raised by commissions of array. With 8 earls, 55 bannerets, 599 knights and 1,821 esquires, it was somewhat over officered by modern standards. But as only the earls, bannerets and some of the senior knights would actually command sub-units of any size, the ratio of officers to soldiers was not too different from present-day arrangements. The army contained around 2,500 men-at-arms and 2,200 mounted archers, all in retinues or contracted, 5,000 foot archers, 3,000 Welsh spearmen and 1200 *hobilar*s, all arrayed. Each Welsh *vintenar* had an interpreter, as many of the men spoke no English. Given that in battle only the earls and the bannerets would be mounted (so that they could see what was happening) and that all others would fight on foot, then the army would field nearly 8,000 infantry and, with the royal bodyguard (of Cheshire archers), about the same number of archers.

Edward had originally ordered that ships and men should be assembled at Portsmouth and the subsidiary embarkation points by 14 February 1346 but when it became apparent that the ships would not be ready in time this was extended to the middle of Lent (23 March in 1346), then to two weeks after Easter (30 April) when a final delay of two weeks was ordered. Even then, high winds and foul weather meant that embarkation could not begin until July, and the process of loading in the order of 20,000 horses and the last of the fresh rations took several days. As the king was responsible for replacing or paying for horses lost in battle each horse as it was loaded had its description (height and markings such as 'star on forehead, white off pastern' etc), owner and value noted. This latter could vary from a *hobilar*'s hack at £1 to a knight's warhorse at £10. Before the king embarked, the ceremony of handing over the great seals took place on the altar of the church in Fareham, Hampshire. At last, on 5 July the ships with their cargo of men, horses, equipment and stores set sail from their respective ports to rendezvous off the Isle of Wight. Once the entire fleet was assembled messengers were sent to London, Dover, Winchelsea and Sandwich with the royal command that no one was to be permitted to leave the country for eight days, a measure intended to prevent French spies from reporting the movement of ships, that could hardly be concealed from watchers on the land. The fleet now headed for France. Edward III was about to earn his place as one of England's greatest soldier kings.

When Edward with his army and fleet left the Isle of Wight, he had a number of possible courses open to him. He could have landed in Flanders, where since the Battle of Sluys the inhabitants were firmly allied to the English, or in Aquitaine where Henry,

Earl of Derby and Lancaster was holding out against French depredations, or in Brittany to join with the troops already there under command of Sir Roger Manny. In all of those locations friendly troops could have ensured an unopposed landing and a secure base whence to advance inland. In the event Edward chose none of these obvious courses but instead elected to land where there were no friendly troops, in a province that was steadfastly French, and whose ruler was Philip VI's son. Edward would of course have been well aware that Philip would be expecting an invasion, but it was imperative that he concealed the actual landing zone and so he headed for Normandy. To land in Normandy was certainly taking a chance, but not so much of a chance as might initially appear, for while there would be no friendly troops to meet him there would be no enemy ones either, as most had been sent off to Aquitaine. By opening up yet another front he would force the French to disperse their forces even more, and prevent them from concentrating. Added to that was the richness of the Norman countryside and of its cities. The former, with the harvest just in, would provide provisions in plenty while the latter would yield rich pickings in plate, jewels, coin and ransom. The sea-borne journey from England to Normandy was highly unpleasant for the men involved, trying to avoid being sprayed by each other's vomit[*] – for just about everyone was seasick to a greater or lesser degree – surrounded by increasing piles of horse droppings and having to try to feed and groom the increasingly fractious animals. Bad weather blew the fleet back almost all the way to the coast of Cornwall before the winds changed, and having left the English ports on 5 July it was not until 12 July that the ships sighted the Norman coast and began to disembark in the bay of La Hougue (now St Vaast-La-Houge) on the eastern side of the Cotentin peninsula. It took three days to land the men, horses and stores. While unloading was going on, ships that had discharged their cargo moved to Barfleur, three miles up the coast, where the sailors found and destroyed seven French warships, before setting fire to the town itself, having first removed all portable valuables.

---

[*] But not horse vomit, for horses have no upchuck facility.

A few disaffected Norman knights appeared and threw their lot in with the English, and their local knowledge would be useful, for time was now of the essence.

Edward was intending to embark upon a chevauchée, literally a 'mounted raid', which involved moving rapidly through enemy territory doing as much damage as possible but avoiding pitched battle. The purpose was partly economic and partly to terrorise. The destruction of property, the levelling of buildings, the reduction of fortifications, the burning of crops, the removal of gold and silver, and the killing of people all damaged the economy by reducing the amount of tax that could be levied while at the same time enriching the invading army. Terror could persuade the population to change its allegiance and spelled out a message to the enemy ruler: come to terms or this goes on and will be repeated. Particularly relevant too, at this period in history, was the damage to Philip's honour and reputation if he could be shown to be incapable of defending his subjects. Leaders of such raids usually aimed to start from a secure base and slash and burn their way to another secure area, or to a port where they could re-embark, before an avenging army caught up with them. Edward would have been intending to sweep up from Normandy to the English county of Ponthieu, at the mouth of the River Somme, and then either return to England or move into friendly Flanders depending upon the French reaction. At the time there was little distinction between enemy soldiers and enemy civilians, indeed the line between them was blurred when most males had a military obligation. Although there was still a vestige of chivalry present in the relations between the nobility of either side, this was rarely extended to their inferiors. The peasant was always the victim in these raids, and nobody, whether English or French, cared very much about him (or her).

By 18 July the English army was all ashore, and that day it moved to Valognes, eleven miles away. On the next day it struck for Carentan, another twenty miles away but was held up at the River Douvres where the locals had destroyed the only bridge. Infantry and cavalry could of course cross the river without too much of a problem, bridge or no, but for the baggage train of wheeled vehicles which carried the tentage, stores, rations and accumulated loot a bridge was needed. Many of the Norman bridges were of stone, which would have taken time and energy to destroy, so many had one span in wood, that could easily be demolished when necessary – and as easily repaired. Edward's engineers rebuilt the bridge during the night and on 20 July the English were in Carentan where a large quantity of provisions and wine fell into their hands. They then burned the town and next day reached the River Vire, where again the bridges giving access to St-Lo had been torn down. Again, the engineers repaired one of the bridges and on 22 July St-Lo was in English hands and again was put to the torch, but not before 1,000 butts of wine had been confiscated. Edward was particularly infuriated by finding the heads of three Norman knights on pikes above the main gate – they had been captured fighting for Edward in Brittany and executed as traitors. Edward's view was, of course, that they had been fighting for their rightful king – him – and in any event one just did not execute captured knights. Bayeux escaped the fate of the other towns on the army's route: its citizens had taken the precaution of sending emissaries pledging allegiance to Edward well before the army got anywhere near the town.

On 25 July the army was approaching Caen, a city bigger than any in England except London, having covered ninety miles in seven days, very fast going when the delays in bridging the rivers and plundering the towns and villages for miles either side of the route are considered. The advance would have been led entirely by mounted knights, men-at-arms and archers, while the foot-borne elements would have followed on, and if the engineers (carpenters and masons) were on foot, as they probably were, then they had made excellent progress indeed. A portion of the dismounted troops had been left behind to support the fleet, which now moved along the coast with the soldiers moving parallel to it, looting and burning every coastal village and farmstead until from Cherbourg to Ustrem (Ouistreham) there was not a house standing nor a farm animal alive, while any stores of grain or other provisions not loaded onto the ships were burned. The purported reason for this devastation was to destroy French naval power in the Channel, to which it undoubtedly contributed, but there was a personal profit motive too. Discipline in the navy was clearly not what it should have been, for despite orders that all ships were to remain in Norman waters some of the crews, having loaded their ships to the gunwales with loot, took off for England to realise their newfound wealth.

Caen was a much more formidable obstacle that the towns captured so far, which had been defended only lightly or not at all. The city itself was centred on William the Conqueror's castle. This was an immensely strong fortification but the town below it was not well suited to defence, as its eleventh century walls were by now in disrepair and in some places falling down. To the northeast and southwest of the castle and about 800 yards from it were respectively the Abbaye aux Dames and the Abbaye aux Hommes, the latter the burial place of William the Conqueror. The commercial heart of the city and its most prosperous suburb lay nine hundred yards south of the castle on the Ile St Jean, centred around the church of St Jean, which is still there, and was unwalled but entirely surrounded by the waters of the Rivers Odon and Orne and their branches.

For days refugees had been pouring into Caen and by the time the English army had reached Fontenay le Pesnel, just east of Tilly sur Seulles, about twelve miles from Caen, the Constable of Caen, the garrison commander, knew that death and destruction were coming his way, and coming soon. He had perhaps 1,200 soldiers, men-at-arms and mercenary crossbowmen recruited from Genoa, and decided to hold only the castle and the Ile St Jean. To abandon the old city was sensible enough – its walls would not have stood an assault even if he had sufficient men to cover all the approaches which he did not – and while both Abbayes were stoutly walled he considered that he could not afford to attempt to hold them. That night an English friar and professor of theology, the Augustinian Geoffrey of Maldon, arrived at the old walls with a letter from Edward. In it, the king promised to spare the lives and goods of the citizens if the city would surrender to him. The council of Caen rejected the demand, the Bishop of Bayeux tore up the letter and the wretched Geoffrey was flung into the castle jail.

CRECY

The English army, divided as was customary into three divisions, or battles, marched at first light and drew near to Caen at mid-morning. The Vanguard, commanded in theory by the Prince of Wales, took possession of the Abbaye aux Dames to the northeast, while the main body, commanded by the king, formed up around the Abbaye aux Hommes, with the third division somewhere north of the castle. Edward now prepared to reconnoitre the city prior to formulating a plan for its capture, when events overtook him. Some soldiers of the Prince of Wales's division, seeing an undefended gate in the eastern walls of the old city made a rush for it and having got there realised that beyond it the city itself was deserted, all the garrison and most of the occupants having decamped to the Ile St Jean. The Earl of Warwick, supposedly the Prince of Wales's adviser and in reality the commander of the division, led more troops into the old city. He was unable to prevent the men from beginning to loot the empty houses and setting those that did not look as if they offered rich pickings on fire. What had begun as an accidental encounter now developed into a full scale assault which spread to the Ile St Jean. There the fighting was particularly brutal in the narrow streets and inside houses, and while the men-at-arms would accept the surrender of a nobleman or an obviously prosperous civilian, the archers and spearmen were in a bloodlust and killed indiscriminately. French knights, conspicuous by their armour and rich trappings, would seek out an English knight to surrender to, knowing that only then would their lives be assured. The castle was never captured and simply ignored. By late afternoon it was all over, and the looting began. It was said that 5,000 French were killed, that 2,500 French bodies lay on the streets and in the houses, stripped and disfigured so that they were unrecognisable, that 500 bodies were buried in a mass grave in the grounds of the church of St Jean, that 250 knights and esquires and a large number of rich merchants were taken prisoner, and that only one English esquire died of wounds some days later. The figure of the French dead is almost certainly too high, while the number of English dead is too low.

The English stayed at Caen for five days. Once the army was back under control, after an initial orgy of plunder and rape, it could replenish its baggage train, collect the valuables of Caen, tend to its wounded, and bury the dead. Those of a less rapacious nature could go and gaze at the tomb of the Conqueror. English, and later British, armies would gain a reputation for misbehaviour on capturing a town, a reputation that would last until well into the nineteenth century. But as English soldiers tended to look for alcohol first and women second, the incidence of rape was generally less than that practised by other nationalities, and hangovers, rather than the threat of the hangman, usually brought soldiers back to their allegiance relatively quickly. While pausing at Caen Edward sent orders back to England for the arraying of 1,200 archers, mainly from East Anglia, and directed that contracts should be let for 2,450 bows and 6,300 sheaves of arrows. Not all the men and equipment would have been battle casualty replacements, but some of them surely were. At the same time 100 ships were to be impressed to replace those that had deserted, and the prisoners were sent off to England from Ouistreham under the guard of the Earl of Huntingdon and a detachment of archers.

Prisoners of rank were an important asset in medieval warfare, for they were the equivalent of prizes for the eighteenth and nineteenth century navy. A man who could afford it was held for ransom, and not released until his family or his subjects had paid up. While the practice of holding men for ransom was a very old one, neither the Welsh not Scottish wars produced very much profit for those taking a prisoner – blood and stones, feathers and frogs spring to mind – but the Hundred Years War was a very different matter. Rich burgesses who had little money could buy their freedom with furs, jewels or plate; rich knights for money; poorer ones for horses or armour or land; and knights with nothing at all might actually agree to serve their captor for a laid down period of time. Arrangements for the allocation of ransom money were usually specified in the indentures, and could range from one third to one half payable to the man's lord. In the contract companies the rule was that the man handed over one third to his captain, who in turn handed over one third of his accrued takings to whomsoever he was contacted (usually the king). Prisoners could also be sold on by a captor who wanted instant cash or who did not want to be responsible for looking after the prisoner through the often many-years-long process of extracting the ransom. Some of the ransoms demanded, and paid, were very high indeed. At Caen, the Constable, the Count of Eu, surrendered to Sir Thomas Holland, who then sold his prisoner to the King for £12,000, or about £9 million today – he ultimately extracted a lot more than that for the release of the count. Sir Thomas Daniel, who took the surrender of the Lord of Tancarville, the Chamberlain of Caen, was less fortunate: as he was a member of the Prince of Wales's retinue, he had to hand his prisoner over, and had to be content with £666 down and a pension of £26.13.4 per annum for life – not bad, but hardly beyond the dreams of avarice. The prince eventually got £6,000 to release Tancarville.

The army was now ready to move on, and Edward had ordered that the recently impressed 100 ships and the archer reinforcements were to rendezvous with him at the port of Le Crotoy, in Ponthieu, which gave the king the option of taking the army off should the situation warrant. Initially, the army marched east, burning and looting as it went.

Philip had already made a half-hearted attempt to negotiate when a French bishop was sent to offer Edward the county of Ponthieu and the confiscated bits of Aquitaine, provided that Edward would hold them as a vassal of the (Valois) King of France, which was of course quite unacceptable. Edward's army crossed the Seine by a reconstructed bridge at Poissy and marched north. The advance guard was commanded by Sir Godfrey de Harcourt with 500 men-at-arms and 1,200 archers, all of them mounted, when they ran into a French army marching south. These were the troops provided by the city of Amiens marching to Paris as ordered, and although they put up a stout defence, they were no match for the now battle-hardened, or at least massacre-hardened, Englishmen. Many of the Amiens burgesses were killed or taken for eventual ransom, but of more importance was the capture of their baggage train which was well stocked with rations, wine and clothing.

The next stop for the army was Beauvais. Here the usual looting and burning was entered into with gusto, but the Abbey of St Lucien was also set on fire, whether deliberately (probable) or by accident (less likely) is not known. As Edward had issued orders that no church buildings were to be damaged, he was not pleased and ordered the hanging of those responsible, said to number twenty but in all probability a lot less than that – soldiers were expensive assets and could not easily be replaced just yet. It is likely that the punishment was dealt out to one or two known bad-hats as a warning that while plundering and burning was officially encouraged, discipline was still required, and men were not to overstep the mark.

The army moved on. By now most of Edward's foot soldiers were mounted on captured Norman horses, but even so, the constant halts to plunder, and the need to forage far and wide for food for the men and fodder for the horses slowed the English down. It was now imperative to get across the Somme and either join with the fleet or head for Flanders, where an allied army had just taken the town of Bethune, but the major bridges were in Amiens and Abbeville. Both these towns were strongly held by French troops, and the main French army commanded by Philip was moving into Amiens. In just over six weeks the English army had covered four hundred miles – considerably more for the foragers and looters – and was now tired, short of provisions, and for the first time in the campaign beginning to encounter partisans. They made little difference to the course of the war but were a nuisance and meant that sentries had to be doubled and the size of patrols increased. The army intended to cross the Somme at a ford at Blanchetaque at first light but a delay in loading the baggage horses and waggons meant that they did not get there until late morning when the tide was in. Not only that but a French force of around 600 men at arms and crossbowmen were waiting on the other side. Then, sometime after Prime (0900 hrs), the tide had gone out sufficiently for the Earl of Northampton to lead 100 men-at-arms and about the same number of flanking archers into the river. The Genoese crossbowmen began to loose their bolts which caused some casualties until the archers got within range. Once the archers began to shoot from about 150 yards the balance shifted, and the English had more men across than the French had to oppose them. The French commander ordered a retreat to Amiens, which soon became a rout as the English men-at-arms mounted their horses and pursued the fleeing French almost to the gates of Amiens. By the time detachments of the main French army arrived at the southern end of Blanchetaque, Edward's army with its men its horses and its wagons – including its accumulated loot – was long gone, the tide was in again and pursuit was impossible. On the evening of 24 August, the French army returned to Abbeville to cross the Somme there, while the English camped in the forest of Crécy.

Chapter Five – The Battle

There can be little doubt that Edward III wanted a battle, and he wanted it to be decisive, but he wanted it on his own terms. Ponthieu had been English by inheritance since 1279, even if Philip had confiscated it, and there was an escape route if needed, either to Flanders or to the coast where he could have rendezvoused with as much of the navy as had not deserted to realise their plunder. Most important of all, there was a possible battlefield that fitted all the requirements of English battle procedure shaped from the experiences of Bannockburn, Dupplin Moor and Halidon Hill. There has been some debate amongst historians as to the exact location of the battlefield of Crécy. On the assumption that everyone knew where a battle took place, chroniclers writing at the time tended not to give more than a cursory description of the location – being more concerned with embellishing tales of knightly chivalry – and archaeology is usually absent. Only when firearms appear on the battlefield can archaeology, by finding where a line of musket balls has landed and therefore from where they were fired, work out fairly accurately what happened. Metal detecting enthusiasts are often surprised that arrowheads, broken swords, spurs, discarded helmets and the like are rarely found on a medieval battlefield. However, arrows, broken swords and the like are valuable items, which can be recycled, and if the field was not thoroughly gleaned by the victors it would be by the local inhabitants, so that in a very short space of time no artefacts would be left.[*] The only evidence for the traditionally accepted site of the battle, apart from what the chroniclers report, which can be read in several ways, is in local tradition and in place names. But the overwhelming argument for accepting the area of the gently sloping valley to the northeast of Crécy-en-Ponthieu as the site of the battle is that if Edward wanted

---

[*] The exception is Towton 1461, but that was fought in a blinding snowstorm over sodden ground and much detritus was trampled into the ground to be discovered by historians and archaeologists much later.

a battle (and all the available evidence is that he did), then he could not have found a better place to have it, assuming that he would want to force the French into attacking him – as English tactical doctrine said he should. There is simply nowhere else within a day's march – and the French were but a day's march behind – that offers anything like the advantages of the Crécy position.

Between the villages of Crécy and Wadicourt running northeast is a ridge along which runs the modern D 111, and which is the side of a valley (the *Vallée des Clercs*) that slopes northeast to southwest between the ridge and the village of Estrées lès Crécy just off a Roman road that is now an extension of the Chausée Brunehaut. Behind the ridge was a wood, and running from Crécy southeast along the side of the valley is the River Maye, while on the northern side of the valley was a steep bank. Assuming that the French would approach from the south or the southeast, it was a perfect defensive position. Edward's army spent the night of 24 August 1346 in and around the woods south and west of the ridge of Crécy. On the morning of 25 August, the king and his senior commanders recced the ground on horseback, looking at every possible line of approach. The plan was simple: the army would take position on the ridge, and dare the French to drive them off it. The strength of Edward's army at Crécy, like that which landed at La Hougue, is and has been the subject of much debate. Edward started off from England with around 16,500 all ranks, all arms. There had not been a pitched battle so far but there would have been a steady attrition from the storming of small towns, the killing of foragers by grumpy farmers, the battle for Caen, and the crossing at Blanchetaque, to say nothing of men wounded and unable to re-join the banners, accidents (there are reports of burning houses collapsing on top of the arsonists), disease, sickness, and desertion. On top of that must be deducted the escort to the prisoners, sent back to England under the Earl of Huntingdon. While it can only be a very rough approximation, it does not seem unreasonable to allow for a reduction in the size of the army of between ten and fifteen percent. As the knights, esquires and men-at-arms were rather better protected than the rest, we might suggest a reduction of ten percent in that category and fifteen percent of the archers and spearmen. Most of the *hobilar*s, not overly involved in skirmishing so far, probably survived. If the foregoing is anywhere near correct and assuming that the majority of the knights fought as armoured infantrymen with the earls and bannerets commanding subunits of varying size, then Edward at Crécy could field 4,428 armoured infantry and 3,900 light infantry, assuming that the *hobilar*s, whose mounted role would now be in abeyance, fought as spearmen (they were equipped with a lance, sword and helmet), and rather more than 3,000 archers.

The army was still in its three battles of roughly the same size, and again there is much debate as to how they were formed up. We can dismiss the suggestion that the soldiers formed up and fought in their mixed arm retinues. This would make no sense, diluting as it would the battle-winning arrow storms, and creating weaknesses in the infantry line. Far more likely it is that, for all the advantages of fighting alongside men they knew and had marched with, the archers must have been separated from the men-at-arms and the light infantry. Although some contemporary accounts have all three battles in line, and some have them one behind the other, neither makes much military sense. It would be unusual to have all three battles in the front line, for there is then no depth to the position – if the enemy pierce the line there is nothing behind to stop them. Similarly, if all three battles are engaged simultaneously there is no reserve, and a commander without a reserve is unable to influence the battle once it begins. The placing of the battles one behind the other reduces fighting power considerably and would be unlikely to cover the frontage. The length of the ridge along which Edward arrayed his army is about 1,500 yards, which allowing room for the archers and gaps between subunits, would need 2,400 infantrymen if formed up two ranks deep, and 4,800 in four ranks. The frontage could only be covered by one battle if the men were formed in two ranks, and this seems most unlikely: it would not be sufficient to withstand the shock of an assault by mounted or dismounted men. If the chronicles and the paintings can be relied upon at all (doubtful, I accept) then the description of hand-to-hand fighting would indicate that the men were formed in at least three and probably four ranks, which would predicate two battles forward. If we rely on the theory of inherent military probability, and what we can extract from the sources, then the most likely deployment seems to be two battles forward in four ranks, the Vanguard of the Prince of Wales on the right as the senior commander next to the king, and the Rearguard under the Earl of Arundel on the left, with the Centre, commanded by the king, in rear. While the three battles were given the titles Vanguard, Centre and Rearguard this did not mean that they necessarily occupied those positions (yet another delightfully confusing aspect of medieval warfare!). As the king was in overall command it made sense for him to be in the rear, where he could control the battle, see what was happening overall, and be able to deploy his battle as a reserve or reinforcement as necessary. In the event, he was able to make use of a windmill on the ridge as a command post, from where he could look over the two forward battles, and easily deploy the rear one if necessary.

As for the archers, here too there is discussion as to deployment. It has been suggested that the archers were formed in line in front of the infantry. This again makes little sense: they would impede the infantry, cause chaos as they tried to avoid a closing enemy and the formation would dilute the effect of their shooting. There can be little doubt that the archers were placed as they were at Dupplin Moor and Halidon Hill, that is on the flanks where their shooting could prevent any outflanking move, force an enemy to close into his centre, and reduce his momentum so that if he did get as far as the infantry line he could easily be repulsed. What is more problematical is whether or not there were archers in the centre as well as on the flanks, for if each battle was allocated its own archers, then it is perfectly likely that archers were positioned on the flanks of each battle. In that case, some would be in the centre of the English line. In most paintings and in many of the original sources the archers are shown or described as being in a wedge shape, and as the commander or commanders of the archers would have to balance the concentration of arrows with the area over which they fell, then a square formation would seem best. If there were 1500 or so archers on each flank, then they could be formed into two squares each of 38 men across and the same deep. If each man occupied a circle with a radius of two yards, room for him to place his arrows on the ground and draw his bow, then each square would need a frontage of around 75 yards; in the heat of battle, the square might well become a lozenge or a wedge. If archers were deployed on the flanks of the battles, rather than on the flanks of the army, then each battle would be flanked by squares each of around fifty yards across, and to an oncoming enemy it would appear that the mass of archers was in the centre of the front line. On balance it would seem likely that the archers were on the flanks of the army only, but one cannot dismiss the possibility that there were some in the centre as well.

Having ridden round the area and decided upon his plan of action, the king ordered pits and holes to be dug across the cavalry approaches, and then had them covered in grass and scrub to conceal them. He had the baggage wagons drawn into the woods of Crécy-Grange on the north side of the ridge where they were used to form a laager, inside which were put the army's horses. As there may still have been as many as 20,000 horses, any lost having been more than compensated for by those captured or plundered, the stabling area would have been enormous. There was neither time nor materials to build stalls, so hitching rails would have been put up. In order to prevent horses from fighting or kicking each other they would have had to have been tied up a good twelve feet apart, with rails eight feet behind each other. This indicates an area of 500 yards by 400 yards for stabling alone, and the animals would have to be fed and watered, a labour-intensive task which would have been partly done by non-combatants and by some of the *hobilar*s, detached to guard the laager and look after the horses at the same time. By morning on 26 August, all was ready. The soldiers heard mass and the priests heard confessions, and the men were told to sit or lie down in their positions while breakfast[*] was cooked by fatigue parties and brought up to the lines.

---

[*] Possibly a potage of stewed vegetables, but more probably bread and cheese washed down with ale.

CRECY

Meanwhile the French army under Philip spent the night of 25 August at Abbeville. As with the English army we can only make an educated guess as to its strength: all sources, English and French, agree that the French were far more numerous than the English. However, their heavy cavalry (composed of the nobility) is variously reported as numbering from 12,000 to 30,000, the (mounted) men-at-arms from 60,000 to 100,000 and the crossbowmen from 2,000 to 15,000. The lowest multiple given by any of the chronicles is that of Le Bel who says that there were four times as many French as there were English. If we err on the conservative side and take a multiple of three, and if we accept that it is most unlikely that Genoa and northern Italy could have produced more than 2,000 crossbowmen at Crécy, and given that they also found garrisons in other parts of the French lands, then we might hazard a guess at the French army consisting of 24,000 heavy cavalry and mounted men-at-arms in the probable proportion of one noble to four men at arms, and 2,000 crossbowmen. Not all those men would have been at Abbeville on the evening of 25 August: units and retinues kept arriving during the night and into the next day.

Philip knew that the English were somewhere in the vicinity of Crécy and on the morning of 26 August the French army began to move north in that direction. Ahead of them went a small recce party of four knights to report the location, strength and intentions of the English. They reported back that the English army was deployed on the ridge between Crécy and Wadicourt, that they looked as if they were prepared for a battle and that there were no indications that they might move off. Furthermore, said the leader of the recce party, would it not be a sensible idea for the French army to concentrate and rest until the following day, when they would be in a much better position to destroy the English upstart? This very sound advice was echoed by Philip's senior commanders and accepted by him. Many French units were still on the march from Abbeville, others were still coming in from other parts of the country, and a large allied contingent from Savoy would not arrive until sometime the following day. Philip was always a cautious commander – in hindsight too cautious perhaps

– but he was absolutely right to heed the advice given and to issue orders that the army was to advance no farther but to bivouac and be prepared for battle the next day. By now the leading French units had reached the *Vallée des Clercs*, about 1,000 yards from the English position. They could see the English and the English could see them. It was late in the day – probably not as late as Froissart thought, Vespers, or dusk – but probably 1700 or 1800 hours, and the English would have been watching more and more French soldiers of various types crowd onto the field. Even the stupidest spearman could do the maths, but as King Edward rode along the lines shouting words of encouragement, his men were quite confident in their ability to hold off the French host.

As Philip's orders to hold hard were delivered to the troops in the vanguard, they obediently halted, but as the orders were relayed farther back the recipients were unhappy: they wanted to get forward where they could see the enemy, and then they might halt. The result was a scrum of major proportions as those behind pushed and shoved to get forward, and those in front tried to hold their positions. In an aristocracy-heavy army where every man felt himself the equal of every other, and instant obedience to orders was an extraordinary concept, there was a general feeling of wanting to get on with the battle – at least amongst the mounted element who had let their horses do the work of the march from Abbeville. It was soon apparent to Philip and his marshals that the task of holding the army back was an impossibility, and so the battle might as well start now. The crossbowmen were ordered forward to lead the advance.

Unlike archers, who except at very close range shot their arrows at a high angle and so could be arrayed in ranks all shooting at the same time, the crossbow was a flat trajectory weapon, and its operators could only shoot one rank at a time. Tactically the intention was that volleys of bolts from the crossbowmen would so disorganise the enemy line by killing large numbers that it would be easy prey for a charge by the mounted knights and men-at-arms. While exact details as to how this missile screen was supposed to act are sketchy, it is logical to suppose that they would have acted in the same way as men armed with matchlocks in a later age. If the rate of discharge was two quarrels a minute, the front rank could discharge its weapon and then move to the rear to reload while the next rank stepped forward and did the same. A formation three ranks deep could therefore loose a volley every ten seconds. If the French army's crossbowmen did advance in this way, then allowing a yard of front per man the 2000 crossbowmen would have covered a frontage of around 700 yards. In view of what happened to them, it is likely that they did not bring their *pavisse*s with them onto the ground – they may have still been in the baggage train, or it may be that they as they were told to move forward, rather than shooting from a defensive line, the shields were too cumbersome to move.

The trumpets sounded and the drums pounded as the crossbowmen began to move towards the English line. Crossing the floor of the valley and beginning to climb the gentle slope they would have halted as soon as they were within range, perhaps 200 or 250 yards away. The English probably allowed them to discharge their first one or two volleys, but shooting uphill and with the setting sun in their eyes, they cannot have hit very much. Then the English archers replied. The captains and the *vintenar*s would have bellowed 'nock – draw – loose' and the deadly arrow storm began. Even thirty seconds seems an age when being shot at, and in that first thirty seconds, the astonishing number of 15,000 arrows would have come raining down from the sky. The archers did not have to hit a specific target, they simply had to ensure that their arrows landed within what a later age would describe as a beaten zone, an area that encompassed the lines of crossbowmen. Relatively densely packed as the Genoese would have been, it is not unreasonable to posit that one in three arrows hit something. That being so, it would not have taken very long before the crossbowmen were thrown into confusion, some dead, many wounded and with no cover and no escape except backwards. They were not helped by one of those sudden and violent summer thunderstorms common in that part of France, accompanied by heavy rain which would have caused their bowstrings to stretch, thus reducing considerably the propulsive power of their weapons.* As standing still and shooting back would have been suicide, those at the rear and able to move found their retreat blocked by the packed lines of mounted knights, while the evident chaos and, to French eyes, cowardice of these despised foreign and low-born mercenaries encouraged the commander of the leading French battle, the Count of Alençon, to order a charge.

Whether he actually ordered his men to ride over the crossbowmen, as some of the chronicles allege, or whether what happened was simply collateral, is irrelevant: the wretched crossbowmen could not get out of the way of big heavy men on heavy horses, and many were trampled underfoot or knocked flying. A horse will go to almost any lengths to avoid stepping on anything alive but packed closely as they were and with head and face armour that restricted their vision, the animals had little option.† Allowing three feet of frontage per horse, that first French charge may have begun with three to four hundred riders, but having negotiated their way past the fleeing crossbowmen or galloped through them, cohesion was lost. Instead of coming on in a controlled line at the canter, they were now a mob of individuals all anxious to strike the first blow. And then the arrow storm began again. Clouds of arrows coming down at an angle out of the sky might not have killed many riders, but it would unnerve them, and it would certainly panic their horses. The force which an arrow would hit could itself knock a rider off his horse even if it did not penetrate his armour. Again, an arrow whacking into a horse's unprotected quarters would not kill it, but it would be very likely to make it rear and dump its rider, or whip round, bolt and take him into the next county, and that is exactly what happened. Those riders who managed to stay aboard and keep their horses pointing

---

* It would of course have had the same effect on the longbowmen's bowstrings, but it takes only a few moments to change the string on a longbow (and archers carried spare bowstrings, usually coiled inside the hat or helmet, hence the expression 'under your hat') and much longer to replace it on a crossbow.
† Stand by a fence at a National Hunt race meeting and see how the horses twist and turn in mid-air to avoid fallen jockeys.

in the right direction had to be lucky to negotiate the camouflaged trenches and pits and then had to face archers shooting directly at them. At 100 yards or less a bodkin point would go through armour or with a bit of luck could penetrate through the slits in the visor and kill the wearer.

The French launched charge after charge, and the archers shot volley after volley, with runners replenishing arrows from the baggage train. As more and more Frenchmen fell and more and more terrified loose horses galloped screaming hither and thither, what had originally been a smooth and open approach to the English line became an obstacle course of dead and wounded men and horses, while Welsh spearmen laid down their lances to come out and kill the wounded. Some French men-at-arms did get as far as the English lines, and occasionally fighting was fierce but the defence line held, and the polearms wrought great slaughter amongst those unlucky enough to be hooked by them. Edward had specifically said that the dead were not to be looted and that no prisoners were to be taken – he did not want to risk men leaving the line tempted by fat ransoms. We can probably dismiss the tale of a knight of the Prince of Wales's retinue coming to the king and asking for help as his son was hard pressed, to be met by a refusal and the admonition 'let the boy win his spurs'. It is surely inconceivable that the king would refuse to support the sixteen year old heir to the throne when he had an uncommitted reserve to hand. We can probably also dismiss the blindness of the King of Bohemia, whose badge of three feathers and motto *Ich Dien* was adopted by the Prince of Wales and has been the crest of Princes of Wales ever since. John, Count of Luxembourg, King of Bohemia, claimant to the thrones of Poland and Hungary and elector of the Holy Roman Empire lost one eye (from disease) in 1336, but it is almost certain that he could see perfectly well with the other. He was killed at Crécy, aged fifty, supposedly having demanded that his household knights take him into the thick of the battle so that he could strike a blow with his sword. His son was also present but survived (having wisely scarpered when it was evident that all was lost) to become the Holy Roman Emperor Charles IV.

The furious battle went on through the evening, but by the time darkness fell there were precious few French knights or men-at-arms left. Those who had not been killed were slipping away, and even Philip had to accept the hopelessness of the cause when his advisers insisted that he too should quit the field. He went, leaving the Oriflamme of St Denis – the royal banner of the Kings of France, only taken out of the Abbey of St Denis in time of war – abandoned on the ground. He paused first at the chateau of La Broye, where he is said to have hammered on the gate shouting, according to Froissart, *'Ouvréz, Ouvréz, chastelian – c'est l'infortuné roi de France'*. Now in the gloaming of that August night the heralds and the priests moved down into the valley to identify the dead – hence the *Vallée des Clercs*. It was a great and glorious victory. The flower of French chivalry lay dead on the field. While numbers are imprecise it is clear that at least 1,500 and perhaps as many as 2,000 of the nobility were killed, along with many thousands of the infantry levies and crossbowmen. Amongst the dead were at least eight members of the extended royal family, including the Count of Alençon, whose impetuosity was a major contribution to the disaster, the Counts of Blois, Harcourt (whose brother was one of the senior commanders in the English army), and Flanders, and the Duke of Lorraine. Only the figures for the dead English men-at-arms have survived – forty – and we might extrapolate that to perhaps 150 archers and spearmen as well, certainly a remarkably cost-effective battle.

It is easy to say that rather than the English winning the battle the French lost it. Certainly, their lack of cohesion, the confused command arrangements, the failure to allow the whole army to assemble out of sight of the English lines, the misuse of the crossbowmen and the impetuosity of individual commanders and knights were major factors in the result of the battle. That said, the English had deliberately selected a position which allowed them to fight the battle in the way that they did best, with protected flanks, a narrow frontage, the use of missile weapons to break up the enemy assault, and dismounted infantry defence. Commanders who cannot depart the field because they have dismounted can only boost the morale of the soldiers under their command. Above all, perhaps, it was the discipline and teamwork of a professional or quasi-professional army under a respected and charismatic leader that won the day – and would have won the day even if the French had a coherent plan and had been commanded as they should have been.

The English army did not attempt to pursue the remnants of Philip's host as it straggled away towards Amiens on the night of 26 August. They were exhausted and needed time to rest and recuperate. It was not until the following day, a Sunday, when the heralds had completed their grisly task of identifying the dead nobles that they realised the extent of their victory. At least two French contingents arriving to join their army and with no inkling that the battle was over were quickly seen off with more slaughter. But true to the code of behaviour between gentlemen, the body of John of Bohemia was washed and wrapped and sent back to Germany, while those of the princes and the more important nobles were transported to the monastery of Maintenay, ten miles to the north. A truce of three days was also announced to allow the locals to find the bodies of the common soldiery, which were stripped and buried in grave pits in the valley. Spin is not solely a twenty-first century political ploy, and a report of the battle was sent back to England by fast cutter. Somewhat embellished, the account, combined with a report of the capture of Caen, was to be read out in all churches, and in a very short space of time all over England there was genuine delight and pride in the great victory over a hated and feared enemy. Now Parliament and the people might grumble at the prospects of more taxes to keep the war going, but they would pay up for what they could see was an ongoing success.

Meanwhile in Amiens the hunt for the guilty was on, and the fault lay with evil counsellors, corrupt officials, the weather or even the displeasure of the almighty. It was also always easy to blame the foreigners. The Genoese crossbowmen were all traitors and were to be hunted down and killed, and many of them were massacred before it was pointed out that these were valuable assets who might be needed elsewhere, and Philip rescinded his order. In any age, a military commander who cannot identify his mistakes is doomed to repeat them; the French refusal to face facts and recognise that their way of waging war was obsolete in the face of rapid discharge missile weapons and professional dismounted infantry was to cost them dear in the future. It was inconceivable that well born French nobles could be defeated by low born archers – '*gens de nulle value*' as one French chronicler put it – and in any case by refusing to take prisoners for ransom the English were not playing fair, while the behaviour of the Welsh in despatching the wounded was very bad form indeed.

Even at this relatively early stage of the war there were sensible French soldiers who could see why they lost the Battle of Crécy, but any question of adopting the English system of professional men-at-arms backed by archers had to be rejected – the state of French society simply could not allow it. Quite apart from the generally held view amongst those who mattered – the nobility – that warfare was a matter for gentlemen, raising large bodies of archers could not be considered. English society at this time was relatively stable, and it was surprisingly mobile. A good man could rise by service and ability, and later in the war there were men who had joined as very junior men-at-arms becoming army commanders, and even archers being promoted to senior positions and knighted. There was not the resentment and hostility between the various social classes that existed in France. There the social structure was static, and any thought of arming the lower orders with a deadly weapon system could not be countenanced. Apart from the time needed to develop an archer, there was the ever present risk that once so equipped, the peasantry would turn against their betters and slaughter them. In England that could not happen; although there were of course oppressive masters and corrupt nobles, most of the population were happy with their lot and knew that there was always the possibility of advancement by merit.

A stunning and complete victory though Crécy was, it would not end the war – there would be many more battles and much death and destruction to come.

Printed in Great Britain
by Amazon